In Shakespeare's Playhouse

HAMLET

In Shakespeare's Playhouse

Other volumes are in preparation

Maurice Percival

IN SHAKESPEARE'S PLAYHOUSE

BY
RONALD WATKINS
AND
JEREMY LEMMON

HAMLET

DAVID & CHARLES
NEWTON ABBOT · LONDON · VANCOUVER

0 7153 6463 4

© Ronald Watkins and Jeremy Lemmon 1974

Set in 11pt on 13pt Aldine Bembo and printed
in Great Britain by Latimer Trend & Company
Ltd Plymouth for David & Charles (Holdings)
Limited South Devon House Newton Abbot
Devon

Published in Canada by Douglas David &
Charles Limited 3645 McKechnie Drive
West Vancouver BC

CONTENTS

PREFATORY NOTE

In this reconstruction of Shakespeare's play we have aimed to preserve
a sense of the continuity of performance. It is important that the text
of the play itself should be kept constantly in mind: quotations from
the episode under discussion are printed in **bold type**; quotations
from other parts of the play, and from other plays or books, have been
placed inside inverted commas. In the quotations we have made as
little departure from the lineation and punctuation of the early texts as
has seemed compatible with the convenience of a modern reader;
spelling, however, has been modernised. We have quoted stage-
directions only from the Quartos and First Folio, since these, in most
cases, may reasonably be supposed to reflect the practice of performance
in Shakespeare's own playhouse; they are printed as they appear in
the early texts, in italics, and not modernised in any way (except that
we have abandoned the long 's', and the 'i' and 'u' which represent,
respectively, 'j' and 'v').

For those readers who wish to keep Shakespeare's text by them as
they read, we have added in the margin Act, Scene and Line numbers,
as milestones of the play's progress. Since no universally standardised
system of reference-numbering is yet conveniently available, we have
chosen in these and other reference-numbers to follow the *Oxford Standard Authors* edition of Shakespeare's Works (edited by W. J. Craig),
except when, for a particular purpose, another edition is specified.

Superior figures in the course of the commentary refer to the
Notes which are grouped together at the end of the book.

INTRODUCTION

The aim of the present volume (as of the other volumes of the same series) is to reconstruct in imagination a performance of Shakespeare's play in the public playhouse during his lifetime, and thereby to throw the clearest possible light upon the play's overall design and its minute detail. It is the aim of the picture-restorer, to remove the over-painting of subsequent 'improvers' and to seek to reveal the masterpiece as it came from the artist's brush. The principles upon which our reconstruction proceeds are set forth in our Introductory Volume, but we append a brief recapitulation to prepare the reader for a visit to HAMLET, as presented at the Globe in the daylight of a London afternoon in 1601, the year in which (so most scholars believe) this play first took the stage. We ask him to bear in mind certain known facts about the circumstances of Shakespeare's working life, and some conclusions which may be drawn from them:

(1)   During most of the period when he was writing his plays, Shakespeare was an active member of the most successful players' company in London; until late in his career, certainly for several years after the appearance of HAMLET, he was present at, and presumably taking a personal part in, the preparation of his plays for performance.

(2)   The plays were written to be performed by the regular members of the company—the body which was already famous in 1601 as the Chamberlain's Men, and within two years was to be given royal patronage as the King's Men. Shakespeare had individual actors in mind when he first conceived HAMLET. T. W. Baldwin

(*The Organization and Personnel of the Shakespearean Company*, 197, 303) has said of Shakespeare's creative method that 'the play was regularly fitted to the company, not the company to the play' and that his plays 'represent not only his own individual invention but also the collective invention of his company'. So while Burbage's Hamlet was Shakespeare's Hamlet, it is no less true that Shakespeare's Hamlet was at least partly Burbage's.

(3)   The plays were presented in repertory—six different plays, by various authors, in a week—repeated at intervals only as long as they were successful in drawing an audience. These conditions preclude the idea of a director's designing and dressing a play as for a long run; the project of putting on HAMLET would not be conceived in terms of a 'production' as we understand the word today.

(4)   The company was extremely adaptable in performance; it was accustomed to appear at court or on tour, as well as in its own playhouse. The untrustworthy first Quarto text claims that its version of HAMLET was 'diverse times acted by his Highnesse servants in the Cittie of London: as also in the two Universities of Cambridge and Oxford, and else-where'. Nevertheless, the plays were for the most part conceived—at least until the acquisition of the Blackfriars playhouse in 1608–9—for the public playhouses; in 1601 the home of the company was at the Globe. The physical and atmospheric conditions of performance in the public playhouse itself were therefore constantly in Shakespeare's mind as he composed his plays.

(5)   The Globe—'this Wooden O'—was octagonal, polygonal or circular, small but capacious, and open to the skies. While we do not know its precise dimensions, it is safe to assume that the overall diameter was less than 100 feet, possibly as little as 80 feet; and that the diameter of the interior (with which we are chiefly concerned) was considerably less than the 78 feet which is the length of a lawn-tennis court. Yet its capacity was more than 2,000. The performance therefore could touch the extremes of intimacy and public address: Hamlet in soliloquy could whisper to each individual hearer, even in the top Gallery; when necessary, a Claudius or a Fortinbras could dominate the crowded audience with a ceremonial announcement.

(6)   The great Stage (the visible embodiment of Hamlet's image of the earth, 'a sterile Promontory') projected into the audience, which stood or sat on three sides of it. The middle of the front of the Stage was the central point of the whole building. The background of the Stage was formed by the façade of the Tiring-House, behind which the actors attired themselves: in it were set two Doors, one on either side, through which the actors emerged on to the Stage. For much of the time the Stage was treated as independent of this background, as when Fortinbras (in IV.iv) and his token army, who have entered through a Door, are felt to be marching across the Danish country-side; occasionally indeed the Stage represents no specific locality at all.

(7)   The Tiring-House, though the details of its architecture are uncertain, was a permanent feature of the playhouse, familiar and accepted by the audience every time they came to the play. It could therefore be ignored altogether or, if such was the dramatist's wish, its features could be used, described and embodied in the action.

(8)   Because of the proportions of Stage and auditorium, by which an actor could stand at the very central point of the whole play-house, the audience were not detached spectators of a remote picture but engaged participants, often partisans, on the fringe of a live action taking place in their midst. A phrase in Hamlet's farewell address exemplifies this comprehensive identification of the persons on the Stage and his hearers in the playhouse: 'You that look pale, and tremble at this chance, That are but Mutes or audience to this act. . . .' Under Burbage's persuasion, the courtiers of Elsinore and the no less dumb-stricken listeners in the Globe have become one.

(9)   This relationship was emphasised by the fact that the per-formance took place in the neutral daylight of a London afternoon, the audience and the players being in the same light. Elaborate lighting effects and the deliberate directing of light were impossible: atmosphere, therefore, and subtleties of characterisation and shifting moods were created by other means—the gestures and miming of the actors, and the spoken word, often conveying to the mind's eye what the physical eye could not see. In this way the poet and players communicate to us the contrast, in the first sequence of HAMLET,

between the icy darkness of the battlements and the warm brilliance of the court; and in the course of the play we shall see that there are subtler effects of illusion and evocation.

(10) The female parts were played by boy-actors, and the illusion of femininity was created by the same means—the words of the dramatist and the intonations, gestures and miming of the players (not only those who played the female parts but also those who acted with them and spoke to and about them). Both the bewildered innocence of Ophelia and the carnal complaisance of Gertrude were within the scope of these young players, but they were not left wholly to their own resources: again and again it is the poet who helps us to sustain the willing suspension of our disbelief.

Moreover, since, in the absence of precise evidence, our reconstruction involves prudent conjecture, we ask the reader to accept as a setting for all that follows the architectural features of the drawing which appears as our frontispiece. Here he will be able to identify the great *Stage* (the main acting arena); the tall broad *Doors* which are the chief means of access to the Stage from the Tiring-House; the *Windows* above the Doors; the discovery-space between the Doors which (for convenience of reference and without any associative intention) we shall call the *Study*; the inset space between the Windows on the upper level which we shall call the *Chamber*; the two *Stage-Posts* set well forward on the Stage; supported by these Posts, the *Heavens* (the painted canopy overhanging the Stage); and the *Trap-Door* in the centre of the Stage, into which Ophelia's coffin is lowered; beneath the Trap-Door is *Hell*, the cellarage from which the Ghost cries 'Swear' to Hamlet and his companions. If all the world is a stage, so too Shakespeare's Stage, lying between the Heavens (Hamlet's 'most excellent Canopy') and Hell (his father's prison-house) is all the world. Above the Heavens are the *Huts*, from which trumpet and banner summon us to the play and from which more than once in HAMLET peals of ordnance are shot off. All these features we shall bear in mind as we trace the course of the play's action: but while it is easy to over-emphasise the importance of the part played by the minor structural features of the playhouse in the development of Shakespeare's craft, we must never forget that the greater part of the action of each play took place on the bare Stage, and that comparatively little use was made of the other features we have mentioned.

Yet we may isolate three conditions of performance in Shakespeare's theatre which were immutable; and these are of cardinal importance in seeking a full appreciation of his dramatic skills:

(A)   a stage or acting area which projected from its background, and on which the action was three-dimensional, like sculpture, not two-dimensional, like painting; so that the audience was closely involved in the action;

(B)   a background which was permanent and unchanging, always basically the same (with perhaps different hangings for tragedy, comedy or history, and other adjusted features of furniture or properties to suit the play of the afternoon) and architecturally constant. The audience, entering the playhouse, knew what they would see, and could ignore the features of the background, if the dramatist so wished. The excited interest, at the first performance of each new play, would be—what will they turn it into this time?

(C)   a constant and neutral light, embracing players and audience alike, so that illusion of light and darkness, or weather or atmosphere, or subtle characterisation, must be created by the miming, gesture and posture of the actors, and above all by the words which the playwright gave them to speak.

*   *   *

In such conditions we envisage 'The Tragicall Historie of HAMLET, *Prince of Denmarke*' at the Globe in 1601. For our prompt-book, we use a conflation of the Quarto of 1604 (Q2) and the Folio of 1623. Q2 is the longer text, having about 220 lines which are not in the Folio version: on the other hand, the Folio has about 85 which are not in the Quarto. The 1604 Quarto claims to be 'Newly imprinted and enlarged to almost as much againe as it was, according to the true and perfect Coppie'. The claim is clearly a counterblast to the pirated version which appeared in the previous year (Q1, 1603), a puzzling travesty of what the Chamberlain's Men considered to be the 'true and perfect Coppie'. The precise relationship of this First Quarto to the other early texts is not clear. The view that it is a reconstruction (made possibly by an eye-witness) of the play we know from the Second Quarto and First Folio is not universally accepted. Nevertheless, whatever its provenance, reference to its dialogue and especially to its stage-directions, where they are not in direct contradiction to the other texts, has sometimes helped us to guess what took place on the Stage of Shakespeare's playhouse, when a performance of HAMLET (in whatever form) was being given. The Folio version, considerably shorter than the Second Quarto, no doubt represents what became the Company's established practice at a later date. While we draw upon both the good texts in our reconstruction, we reproduce, as far as possible without obscuring the sense, the Folio's punctuation and capital letters. The Folio punctuation cannot with certainty be said to be the poet's own, and several different hands, not least those of the editors, Shakespeare's fellow-players Heminges and Condell, were no doubt concerned in its distribution; yet its purpose seems in many cases to be rhetorical rather than syntactical, preserving the fluency and variety of spoken language, and it is our nearest approach to the diction of the players and the poet's phrasing. The Folio's capitals, though they cannot be analysed to represent a system of emphasis, seem nevertheless to reflect from time to time a sense of thematic proportion. While we have, for the reader's convenience, made occasional changes, and indeed modernised the spelling throughout, we strongly urge interpreters of Shakespeare, player and student alike, to work from the early printed texts: the quiddities of the Elizabethan and Jacobean printing-houses are no great obstacle to the judicious reader, and under the seemingly eccentric variations of spelling, punctuation, lineation, speech-headings, stage-directions, there lie many clues and trails for the detective who would unravel the mystery of what really happened on the Stage of Shakespeare's Globe.

*   *   *

Those who adopt the time-honoured view that we know very little about Shakespeare's life, seem to forget that nearly twenty years of it were spent in the whole-time occupation of the playhouse—not only the penning of plays, but rehearsal, training, discussion, adjustment, explanation, improvisation, experiment; and all this among a company of colleagues who were unique in the long endurance and for the most part amicable relationship of their association. Since the range of our speculation covers not only the afternoons of performance but also the mornings of rehearsal, and even the late-night post-mortems at the Mermaid Tavern, it is part of our brief to become acquainted with Shakespeare's fellow-actors, and to let their names grow familiar in the mouth as household words. For this purpose we step still farther into the field of conjecture, seeking the aid of Professor Baldwin's book which, besides expounding the facts of the company's organisation, is bold enough to dally with surmise as to the casting of roles. Though we may disagree with this or that ascription, the attempt is valuable, because it keeps us in mind of the fact that the members of the Shakespearian company provided among them the first interpreters of these acting roles which are usually discussed as if they existed in abstract independence. We come closer to the circumstances in which Shakespeare conceived his play, if we remember that Burbage was about thirty years old when he created the prototype of all subsequent Hamlets, and had recently had opportunity to develop the varied art of reflective soliloquy as King Henry the Fifth and as Brutus; and that the poet himself first spoke the eloquent periods of the Ghost, and for much of the play was free to watch the action of his fellow-players.

That Heminges's Polonius had predecessors in old Capulet, Richard the Second's Uncle York, Egeus, Glendower, Leonato, is more important to our investigation than the possibility that old Lord Burghley may have provided a model from life. Armin's Grave-digger, that 'absolute' catechist, evolved from a new dimension of fooling, since Will Kemp yielded his place as chief comedian of the company. This play indeed provides a unique opportunity to savour the atmosphere of fellowship in an Elizabethan cry of players. In Hamlet's list of King, Knight, Lover, Humorous Man, Clown and Lady, we are in touch with just such a repertory company as the Chamberlain's Men; we hear, it seems, the playwright's own voice in castigation of gagging clowns and barn-storming tragedians and rowdy groundlings; we hear it too in admiration of a play that is modest and wholesome, and in recognition of the status of players—abstract and brief chronicles of the time, whose business it is to hold the mirror up to nature. By keeping the presence and influence of the individual players constantly in mind, we have a more vivid impression of the poet himself, ready no doubt to listen to suggestion but, because of his standing as a shareholder in the company, and his unique value as a box-office draw, allowed (is it rash to assume?) to have the last word in decision. It is with such a purpose of evoking the atmosphere of Shakespeare's 'workshop' that we print Baldwin's cast-list, disputable though it is, for HAMLET; dating the play in the summer of 1603, rather later than the generally accepted 1601, he allots the parts as follows:

Hamlet	Burbage
Claudius	Lowin
Horatio	Condell
Polonius	Heminges
Laertes	Sly
Ghost	Shakespeare
First Gravedigger	Armin
Osric	Cowley
Rosencrantz	Cooke
Fortinbras	Gilburne
Gertrude	Crosse
Ophelia	Wilson

*　　　*　　　*

Rapid, uninterrupted continuity is an ingrained element in Shakespeare's narrative intention. Such is the impression recorded in almost all the Quarto texts, where a general *Exeunt* is the only mark of the end of a scene, and is followed (with scarcely more than the normal gap that indicates in a prose text a new paragraph) by a new entry. The habitual practice is reflected in the simile used by the Duke of York to describe King Richard's humiliation as he rides into London at the heels of Bolingbroke:

As in a Theatre, the eyes of men
After a well grac'd Actor leaves the Stage,
Are idly bent on him that enters next,
Thinking his prattle to be tedious . . .

The Act and Scene division of the Folio is so incomplete and rudimentary as to imply that it is in the main an uncharacteristic attempt
on the part of the editors to give the volume a literary flavour. 'The
two hours' traffic of our Stage' might well be an assessment more
conventional than realistic of the playing-time of ROMEO AND JULIET,
but the phrase certainly suggests a swiftness of performance we are
unused to in our time. An uncut performance of HAMLET, even of the
shorter Folio version, is rarely to be seen today. A performance of the
kind we present here entails a minimum of digressive 'business', and
a continuity of action depending on a continuity of the 'sound-track'
—the speech of the actors supported by musical effects and sound-
effects of trumpet, drum, hoboyes or cannonade prescribed in the
playwright's score. Shakespeare's swift continuity is reinforced by insistent narrative relevance, which will sometimes (though by no means
habitually) depend on a distribution of scenes between the different
acting areas of Stage and Tiring-House. It is a fruitless quest to seek
for systematic formulas of scene-rotation: improvisatory versatility is
a hall-mark of Shakespeare's genius, and we must never forget that he
and his fellows were often obliged to perform in conditions (at court
or on tour) which were very different in structural detail from those
of the public playhouse. But assuming as we do that Shakespeare
conceived his plays for the public playhouse (which was the home-base
of his company, and a purpose-built instrument for the performance
of his kind of poetic drama) before he faced the problem of adaptation
elsewhere, we believe that a detailed exploration, passage by passage,
of his narrative continuity will advance our purpose of understanding
his dramatic intentions in all their variety. Two sequences especially
in HAMLET seem to be so apt to the architectural complex of Stage and
Tiring-House as to make us wonder which had the greater influence
on the other—the playwright on the playhouse, or the playhouse on
the playwright. The silent Ghost descends from the Chamber, the

platform where the sentries watch (I.iv), to the Stage, where he at last speaks to his son (I.v), and subsequently by the Trap-Door into Hell, where he can 'work i'th'earth so fast', and cry 'Swear' under the Stage. Later in the play, the whole sequence that follows the stampede after the Mouse-trap play—the King at prayer, Hamlet's visit to his mother's closet aloft, the stowing of Polonius's body, the wild descent in a game of 'hide Fox', and the inquisition before Claudius ('you shall nose him as you go *up the stairs* into the Lobby')—all this passage we shall plot in detail in the circumstances of the Globe, and hope to show how vividly the continuity of the narrative is reinforced by the architecture of the playhouse.

*   *   *

The back-stage men were not overworked in the performance of HAMLET. The furniture and properties of the play—whether discovered in Study or Chamber, or planted on the Stage before the beginning of the action or carried out during its course—were of the simplest kind. Some of them are prescribed in stage-directions, some can be deduced from the dialogue: they are either functional or evocative; chief among them are the council-table (I.ii); the double royal thrones for the play-scene; the players' own cart-load of properties; the pick-axe and the spade, Yorick's skull, perhaps a wheel-barrow; the elaborate paraphernalia of the final duel, listed in the various particularity of the stage-directions of Second Quarto and Folio. Such economy, we fancy, was Shakespeare's habit until late in life he yielded to the growing fashion for spectacle. His appeal through the spoken word to the mind's eye of his audience needed no reinforcement of visual realism: when Titania wanted a couch to sleep on, it was the familiar moss-bank from the company's property-store that featured in the discovery-space; but it was Oberon who, by his preliminary description, gave appropriately luxurious beauty to that 'bank where the wild thyme blows'. The same well-worn property reappears in HAMLET, when the Player King lays him down upon *a Banke of Flowers*.

Costume, on the other hand (so the evidence suggests), was sumptuous—at least for the principal figures of the story. Surprisingly large sums were spent on the dressing of Kings and Queens in the Elizabethan theatre, and apart from the purchases which figure in the playhouse accounts, we are told that the nobles at court gave their discarded but still splendid garments to the players. It seems likely that there was no special attempt at period dress for HAMLET. A few hints suggest a contemporary style—Hamlet's doublet and stockings, the boy-player's chopine, the French rapiers and poniards. Others—a sea-gown, a suit of sables, a bonnet—tell of no specific period. But Shakespeare's vision of the circumstances of his story was habitually related to his own times; even in the Roman plays, the powerful evocation of antiquity stands side by side with the details of Eliza-bethan life. In JULIUS CAESAR, for instance, the principal actors probably made some attempt to superimpose classical splendour upon Eliza-bethan nether-garments, but the mob and the common soldiers were no doubt indistinguishable from their compatriot groundlings in the Yard. In this matter of costume in the Elizabethan theatre, we must remember the conditions of a weekly repertory of six plays, and discard all notions of an elaborate comprehensive design for production: improvisation and make-do would be the order of the day. Neverthe-less we may be sure that, as with furniture and properties, Shakespeare's keen eye for dramatic relevance would have played some part in choos-ing the wardrobe. The startling contrast of Hamlet's 'Inky Cloak' with the wedding finery of Claudius's courtiers; the bizarre appearance of his 'Antic disposition', with 'doublet all unbrac'd, No hat upon his head, his stockings foul'd, Ungart'red, and down-gyved to his Ankle'; the Ghost's first martial attire, and the pathetic contrast of his later visit to his widow's closet *in his night gowne* (an appropriate hint which we owe to the First Quarto); the distinctive uniform of Fortinbras's Norwegian army; the dandified caricature of young Osric, the 'water-fly'—all these features have their dramatic importance, and would be emphatically underlined by selection from the company's wardrobe.

*   *   *

And before we begin to describe that early performance of HAMLET at the Globe in the London afternoon, we should take a quick look at the audience who are now gathering in the Galleries and in the Yard.

There in the Yard are the groundlings, 'barren Spectators', who, just because today they will hear themselves described as 'for the most part . . . capable of nothing, but inexplicable dumb shows, and noise', may be thought willing to laugh not only at the clowns who speak more than is set down for them, but (under the raillery of their favourite star, Burbage) at themselves too. There in the Galleries are the inns o' court men, the shrewd-witted lawyers of the *avant garde*, ready to fasten on the finer points of topical satire, to relish Armin's grave-side parody of legal jargon, and the Prince's subtler disquisition on the fate of a lawyer's skull—'Is this the fine of his Fines . . . to have his fine Pate full of fine Dirt?' And there, in the Lords' rooms, are the noble few, whose cultivated sense will appreciate the quality of an excellent play, well digested in the scenes, the 'Judicious' whose single censure must 'o'erweigh a whole Theatre of Others'. The wide-ranging social variety of this audience, no less than the other conditions (atmospheric, architectural, circumstantial) of the Elizabethan playhouse, contributed to the inspiration of Shakespeare's dramatic achievement, and it should dispel the qualms of those many faint-hearts who declare that Shakespeare's plays (in the form in which he left them) cannot cast their spell upon an audience of today.

*   *   *

In the end, we must remember that almost all we have left of Shakespeare is the spoken word of his actors; and the converse of this proposition is no less important, that (because the conditions of his theatre needed the poetic drama) the legacy is complete: as the starting-point of our reconstruction, we need desire no more. But the potent art of Shakespeare's spoken text requires minute and patient analysis. We must understand his *sense*—in plain statement, in irony and paradox, in word-play, in the contest of wit; in HAMLET of all plays the mercurial intelligence of the protagonist is a challenge to our swift and full understanding of verbal manoeuvre. Especially must we avoid the common error of under-rating Shakespeare's precision of language, mistaking for clichés and catch-phrases what are exact expressions. Our ears, habituated to an empty cliché, 'heart of hearts', easily miss the delicacy of the Prince's tribute to Horatio whom he will wear in

his heart's core—'Ay, in my Heart of heart'. We must pay due attention to the *shape* of Shakespeare's text—the balance of word against
word, phrase against phrase; the deliberate antithesis (we shall see how
the device is used in Claudius's first utterance to express the contrived
formality of diplomacy); the characteristic phenomenon of iterance;
the habit by which one speaker picks up and reinterprets the words of
another (as when Horatio cries of the ubiquitous burrowings of the
Ghost that 'this is wondrous strange', and prompts the Prince to fasten
on his word: 'And therefore as a stranger give it welcome': such
subtlety is easily overlooked on the printed page, but Burbage does
not let us miss the reinterpretation). We must attune our ears to the
sound of Shakespeare's text—the underlying iambic stress of pentameter verse, and the common variations and less common distortions
of it; the incompleteness of a line's rhythm, deliberate short lines and
defective lines, such as Horatio's expectant silences as he appeals to
the unresponsive Ghost: 'Speak to me . . .'; the seemingly accidental
assonance; the enrichment of mood and feeling by manipulation of
sound, as when (in Pope's phrase) 'the sound must seem an echo to
the sense'—so Hamlet's disgust is audible in his words, ' 'Tis not alone
my Inky Cloak (good Mother) Nor Customary suits of solemn
Black . . .'; the building climax of a long paragraph; the long running
rhythm which sustains the tension of a whole scene; the effect of variation in metrical pattern and the subtle change from verse to prose
rhythm; the many differing purposes (perhaps clinching, perhaps
ironical or frivolous) of rhyme. Always the sound, the actual com-
bination of vowels and consonants, the long and the short, the quick
and the slow, the sharp and blunt, the heavy and the light weight—the
sound itself is an enrichment of the sense. And apart from the manipulation of sense, shape and sound, the art of Shakespeare and his fellow-
players involved other more conventional *skills*—the handling of
soliloquy, speaking aside, dialect, the representation of character in
speech (Heminges must learn how iteration, indirection and aphorism
express the personality of Polonius)—all however based upon their
handling of the spoken word. And it must be supposed that the
crown of their accomplishment, the skill in which their apprentices
were most rigorously and successfully trained, was the ability to con-

vey to the mind's eye of their audience all the *pictures conjured up in Shakespeare's text*: for of all poets he is the most pictorial. These pictures may take the form of narrative, as when Ophelia describes to her father Hamlet's distraught intrusion into the privacy of her closet; the episode is an integral part of the play's texture. They may take the form of character-sketching, or the description of a momentary mood; or the creation of atmosphere; or figurative imagery, a thumb-nail sketch to illustrate a point, or an extended image. Occasionally by repetition or echo a pervasive image may have a powerful influence on the play's dramatic effect. The actor's task was to make sure that the imagination of his hearers was persuaded to envisage these pictures, these images, which are part of the texture of Shakespeare's play. Only by tracing each sequence, every speech, each line in the context of Shakespeare's playhouse can we recognise the completeness of Shakespeare's play, and appreciate how there is no waste matter, no irrelevance, no superfluous ornamentation in the opulence of this playwright's invention. Moreover this analysis must be made not by arbitrary thematic selection but in the sequence of the play itself as we see it in performance. Confronted with the necessity of creating illusion by poetical means, he has been over every inch of the ground before us. The question we have constantly proposed to ourselves is 'What did the Chamberlain's Men do?' And the summary answer is that they carried out the instructions which are implicit in their playwright's text. In all that follows, we seek to elucidate those instructions. Let it be clearly understood that we are not proposing a definitive performance. There remain large areas of latitude and difference in interpretation. It is our loss that we do not have the playwright himself to watch over us in morning rehearsal. Nevertheless even when our interpretation is open to debate, we hope there is matter enough in this reconstruction to demonstrate the truth of our belief—that there is no need to 'improve' upon Shakespeare's work; that he knew what he was about; that he knew how to make a play.

The Tragedy
of
HAMLET
Prince of Denmark

[I.i.1-18] There are reasons for thinking that the action of the play begins on the upper level of the Tiring-House. More concerned with situation than with precise locality, Shakespeare presents to us 'the Watch': when Hamlet, hearing about the ghostly encounter of this opening scene, asks 'But where was this?' (I.ii.212), he receives the answer 'My Lord, upon the platform where we watch'd'. The upper level has habitually served in the military context of history plays for battlements, which are the natural setting for sentry-go. Both Q2 and Folio identify the occupation of the first speakers: *Enter Barnardo and Francisco, two Centinels.* The atmosphere of the scene is dark, remote, uncanny, in deliberate contrast with the garish splendour of the follow-ing scene at court. The contrast of mood is most clearly marked in a later scene (I.iv) when Hamlet joins the watchers on their vigil: on that occasion the sound of the King's 'wassail' from the state-rooms below accentuates the sinister chill of the battlements above, where 'the Air bites shrewdly' and the time approaches 'wherein the Spirit held his wont to walk'. As on that second encounter, so now we have our first view of the Ghost in the comparative remoteness of the Chamber. Not until he breaks silence (in I.v) is he allowed to come to close quarters with the groundlings.

The means by which the poet prepares us, in less than fifty lines, to see a Ghost in his day-lit theatre, deserve analysis. The Heavens are hung with black for tragedy.[1] A distant clock is striking twelve as the Chamber-curtains open, preparing us for Barnardo's **'Tis now struck twelve, get thee to bed Francisco**. Francisco, the sentinel on guard, emerges from one side of the Chamber, and this side at once becomes associated in our minds with the guard-post. The voice of Barnardo is heard off-stage from the other side:

Who's there?

The fact that the new-comer, not the sentry, makes the challenge, is at once dramatic: Francisco's reply has an emphatic pronoun: **Nay answer me**. The uneasiness of both men (and so too the uncanny atmosphere of the scene) is economically created in the phrases **For this relief** (the last word deliberately ambiguous), **'tis bitter cold** (an effect which will be reinforced by gesture), the strange words **sick at heart . . . quiet Guard . . . Not a Mouse stirring . . . bid them make haste**. That Barnardo is relieving Francisco becomes clearer in the actions of the two men, one taking off his pack as he approaches the guard-post (for he is beginning his watch), the other shouldering his pack before his ears catch the sound of footsteps from the other direction.

[19-40] In response to Marcellus's **Holla**, Barnardo returns from the guard-post. The names are carefully established in the dialogue and dinned in by repetition. **Horatio** especially is forced on our attention, as the philosophical student and sceptic, who

says, 'tis but our Fantasy,
And will not let belief take hold of him . . .

It is he (according to Q2, rather than Marcellus, as in the Folio) who speaks the line **What, has this thing appear'd again to-night?** 'This thing' has a hint of the scholar's irony. The cause of the general nervousness becomes increasingly explicit as **this dreaded sight . . . this Apparition**.

Horatio's scepticism too becomes explicit: **Tush, tush, 'twill not appear**. Nevertheless, at Barnardo's request, they **sit down awhile** and by their sitting compel the attention of the audience to his evocative story. It begins, as ghost-stories should, with the creating of atmosphere: in a long and sinister sentence, launched by the poet with the tantalising half-line of a practised raconteur, Barnardo leads his listeners almost to the point at which yesterday the Ghost appeared:

> Last night of all,
> When yond same Star that's Westward from the Pole
> Had made his course t'illume that part of Heaven
> Where now it burns, Marcellus and my self,
> The Bell then beating one . . .

It is an excellent dramatic contrivance: for the chill Barnardo casts upon his listeners falls upon the audience too, and their flesh is already creeping when (his sentence still incomplete) the story suddenly becomes reality:

> Peace, break thee off:
> Look where it comes again.

[41-69]   The text gives us indication enough of what Shakespeare intended for the Ghost's appearance: later in the play emphasis will be placed upon the pathos of his figure; for the moment, he has

> that Fair and Warlike form
> In which the Majesty of buried Denmark
> Did sometimes march . . .

he is in full armour, his 'beaver' (the visor of his helmet) is raised so that his face is visible, he carries a truncheon (we find these details in the account given to Hamlet by the watchers later in the play), and his gait is a **Martial stalk**. Horatio's scepticism is instantaneously dispelled. As is his habit, Shakespeare interprets for us, in the succeeding words of Marcellus and Horatio, what we have seen. The father, we may assume, wants to make communication with his son: he is, they think, **offended**, perhaps by the strange voices, perhaps by Horatio's challenge, and he **stalks away.**[2] This is, it turns out, the third time he has appeared **jump at this dead hour**, and, so thinks the now convinced Horatio, the portent can only bode **some strange eruption to our State.**

[70-125]   The attention of the audience thus startlingly arrested, the dramatist can now afford to deploy some leisurely exposition. Sitting

once again, and seizing upon Horatio's suggestion that the peace of the state is at hazard, Marcellus fills out with vivid circumstantial detail the picture we have seen of **this same strict and most observant Watch.** But it is Horatio (somewhat surprisingly, since he has only just arrived in Denmark) who is charged with the task of explaining why the country is in a state of emergency. It seems likely that the actor who played this part had special skill in speaking (it was Condell perhaps; we shall see, at the beginning of IV.v, how once again unexpected but effective use is made of this player's skill). Certainly we must be made to listen carefully and digest the political background of the story—the hereditary rivalry between Norway and Denmark and the resolute ambition of young Fortinbras, **of unimproved Mettle, hot and full**—if the tragedy is not to be stripped of its public importance: we are being prepared for a clash between mighty opposites 'upon whose weal depends and rests The lives of many' (III.iii.14 f.). The first scene gives us a strong impression of that political and moral uncertainty, that 'Something . . . rotten in the State of Denmark' (I.iv. 90), the whispered rumours, tortuous diplomacy and ruthless action, which are the essential background for the high tragedy of the Danish court.

We may notice in parenthesis the powerful impression Plutarch has made upon the poet's mind with his account of the portents seen in Rome before Caesar's death: **the sheeted dead** that gibbered **in the Roman streets** had already featured in the text of the recent JULIUS CAESAR: King Hamlet is likewise a **portentous figure.** In the fuller version of Q2 this curious reminiscence returns us to that sense of the ominous which, during Horatio's business-like expounding of the political situation, we have momentarily forgotten.

[126–146]   Since Horatio holds our attention fixed, and his 'sheeted dead . . . in the Roman streets' chill our blood no less than the story with which Barnardo heralded the first appearance of the Ghost, we catch our breath when we see that the Ghost has returned. This time, in spite of danger (**though it blast me**) and the menace of the Ghost's spread arms (Q2 has the explicit stage-direction: *It spreads his armes*), Horatio stands in his path and entreats him to speak. Three times he holds his breath on a half-line. Though the first (*line 129*) is disguised, the second and third pauses are clearly marked in the lineation of Q2. The short lines are rhythmically dramatic, for in the silent pause we hear the iambic clock ticking:

> **If thou hast any sound, or use of Voice,**
> **Speak to me. If there be any good thing to be done,**
> **That may to thee do ease, and grace to me,**
> **Speak to me.**
> **If thou art privy to thy Country's Fate**
> **(Which happily foreknowing may avoid)**
> **O speak . . .**

It might be Horatio's heart-beat, waiting for the answer which does not come. On the cue **Speak of it**, the Ghost lifts up its head, 'like as it would speak', but a distant sound—*The cocke crowes*—causes it to shrink 'in haste away'. (I.ii.217, 219). The contrast between the Ghost's previously majestical bearing and the sudden shrinking, as if in panic, starting **like a guilty thing Upon a fearful Summons**, is pathetic, and the attempt to stop its departure by a **show of Violence** is no sooner made than condemned as **malicious Mockery**.

[147-175] Horatio again interprets for us what we have just seen, telling us how at the cock's warning **Th'extravagant and erring Spirit, hies To his Confine**. The method is characteristic of Shakespeare's poetic drama. Marcellus's beautiful cadenza about the **wholesome** nights of the Christmas season adds a further dimension to the theme of ghost-lore; but it does more than this. A playwright whose method was that of realistic presentation would not have put such a speech into the mouth of Marcellus: with this lyrical and formal language he turns aside from his 'character' and becomes the instrument upon which the poet sounds for his audience the notes of sweetness and wholesomeness.

Horatio continues the process: pointing outwards beneath the canopy of the Heavens, he dispels the night with his unforgettable personification of **the Morn in Russet mantle clad**. The scene began at midnight: now it is dawn: so much has happened in the interval that the transition, in dramatic time, seems natural. With the morning the story must progress: we have seen tonight the apparition of old King Hamlet; **young Hamlet** must be told; for if the Spirit is **dumb to us**, it **will speak to him**. Thus at the cadence of the opening scene, and not till then, the hero of the ensuing tragedy is brought almost casually to the notice of the audience. To him Horatio is bound on two counts, and the Folio's capitals point them for us:

> **Do you consent we shall acquaint him with it,**
> **As needful in our Loves, fitting our Duty?**

Our curiosity is excited in anticipation of the next phase. Moreover this double obligation must be carried out **this morning**.

* * *

[I.ii] *Florish. Enter Claudius, King of Denmarke, Gertrad the Queene, Counsaile: as Polonius, and his Sonne Laertes, Hamlet, Cum Aliis.*

The stage-direction of Q2 suggests that, as soon as the curtains of the Chamber are closed, the Study is opened and a council-table is discovered; in just such a way the third scene of OTHELLO, anticipated by the announcement that 'the Duke's in Council', begins with the Duke and Senators *set at a Table*. Rich hangings in the Study and the bright colours of the garments worn by the courtiers make an immediate and dazzling contrast with the sombre tone of the previous scene. A bustle of preparation, dominated by Polonius, strengthens this sense of a council and from the beginning establishes this privileged councillor's position in the court. But it is not long before our attention is drawn to the incongruously black-clad figure sitting at one end of the council-table. A flourish of trumpets heralds the approach of the King and Queen. The councillors stand to receive their sovereign. Did Burbage delay his rising for a moment, thus reinforcing the note of incongruity? There will be tension and conflict before a word is spoken. All sit, and the royal chairman opens the business of the day.

[1-16] His preface is smiling diplomacy. The sudden death of his brother (of whom Claudius seldom speaks without a calculated epithet of endearment or praise) was cause for general mourning, but discretion has prompted him to a speedy marriage with his widowed sister-in-law, **th'Imperial Jointress to this warlike State**; for it is important that under the threat of war the state should not seem 'to be disjoint, and out of Frame'. After the carefully constructed, smoothly balanced phrases in which he expounds his diplomatic problem, he offers his thanks to his councillors whose **better Wisdoms . . . have freely gone With this affair along.** They have, in fact, acquiesced in the necessity of **mirth in Funeral and Dirge in Marriage.** This mingling of **Delight and Dole** is the climax of a series of deliberate antitheses by which Claudius converts the jarring anomaly of his marriage into pleasantly convincing diplomacy. Meanwhile it is clear to the eye that the acquiescence is not unanimous, because these para-doxical phrases are underlined for us in the contrast between Hamlet's mourning garb and the wedding-finery of the rest of the court. It is possible that Shakespeare (with his habitual directness of narration) means us to see this council-meeting as an immediate sequel to the marriage-ceremony on the day of the wedding itself.

[17-41] From personal matters the King turns to foreign affairs and speaks of the menace from Norway, of which we have already heard from Horatio in the previous scene. Young Fortinbras's uncle, unlike Hamlet's, is **Impotent and Bed-rid** and unaware of his nephew's aggressive purpose. Claudius sends him a peremptory mes-sage of command, **to suppress His further gait herein**, and we do not miss the tone of autocratic authority which underlies his habitual smile. His instructions to the ambassadors emphasise the note of general acquiescence: this court, unlike that of Norway, is conformist and smoothly disciplined, and the Prince's behaviour will seem all the more eccentric for that.

[42-63] With the departure of the ambassadors the interest shifts to Laertes, but not without a momentary glance from the King (and of course we in the audience shall follow his glance) at the mourning figure at the end of the table: if we are seeing the play for the first time, we shall actually not know yet who this still silent person is or why he is so conspicuously, even rudely, unresponsive to his surround-ings. Laertes is interesting not only as a son of the busy old councillor who fusses at his elbow but also because he wants to leave the court.

The indulgent King, no doubt anticipating trouble with his nephew, grants the young man's suit almost before it is presented, promising it as a gift to his loyal and trusted father. Shakespeare's keen ear finds in the name 'Laertes' an opportunity for caressing repetition—**And now Laertes . . . What is't Laertes? . . . What wouldst thou beg Laertes? . . . What wouldst thou have Laertes?** The tone of the young man's request suggests that he does not expect ready agreement, but he cannot **speak of Reason to the Dane** and lose his voice; the reasonable Claudius, charmingly deferring to Polonius, agrees readily enough. Later, when we find that Hamlet wants the same permission, we appreciate the dramatic force of this exchange of petition and ready consent: there is nothing to be lost and something to be gained by indulgence towards the son of the sycophantic Polonius, but his own nephew is not to be given a like licence. Claudius (at *line* 114) expresses his will very clearly: young men at liberty abroad are dangerous to the new regime: 'It is most retrograde to our desire'. Ironically it is Laertes in the sequel (IV.v.88 ff.) who proves only too plainly that the King's instinct was right.

[64-86] And so at last the King turns to the mysterious figure at the end of the table, and the mystery, at least of his identity, is clarified; this is *young* Hamlet (who is to be told 'this morning' what we already know, about his father's ghost walking the night). Four lines of alternate speech are the opening shots in a duel which lasts the length of the play:

—But now my Cousin Hamlet, and my Son?
—A little more than kin, and less than kind.
—How is it that the Clouds still hang on you?
—Not so my Lord, I am too much i'th'Sun.

Shakespeare's compressed exposition is masterly: the King's address not only identifies the Prince but throws into sharp relief his ambiguous relationship—he is both **Cousin** (we should say, nephew) and **Son** (stepson). In the day-lit playhouse the sharp breaking of Hamlet's long silence has almost the effect of showing us his face for the first time. There is disgusted rejection in his opening line, **A little more than**

kin, and less than kind. His wit is immediately at work with riddling retort and incisive word-play. The King's question raises the visible issue of his incongruous clothing; his **nighted colour** becomes the centre of the flamboyant group; he is indeed **too much i'th'Sun**. Burbage does not fail to drive home the secondary meaning—'too much in the S-O-N'—have the goodness not to try to usurp my father's place in my affections! It is interesting that, while the Folio prints 'Sun', Q2 has 'sonne'. Hamlet's rejection of the King's solicitude brings him forward from the council-table in the Study on to the Stage itself, where the rest of the scene will take place: the Prince, seeming so long aloof from the business of the council, no longer remains aloof from the audience; at this moment he becomes the focus of the play's action.

To an audience seeing the play for the first time the purpose of the King and Queen is not immediately clear: that they have a concerted purpose is plain when in turn (he perhaps urging her forward) they each claim the ear of Hamlet. It appears from the Queen's words, and from the beginning of the King's homily, that they are chiefly concerned to persuade him to abandon the ostentatious mourning for a dead father which **seems** to be his particular affectation. Hamlet's indignant answer to his mother has a swooping emphasis—

Seems Madam? Nay, it is: I know not seems—

'Seems ... is ... seems' making a counterpoint of three against the five beats of the iambic pentameter; and in his subsequent denial of the charge of insincere ostentation, the stress of 'k' and 's' sounds forcefully expresses his disgust:

'Tis not alone my Inky Cloak (good Mother)
Nor Customary suits of solemn Black ...

I am not a play-actor, says Hamlet: **I have that Within, which passeth show**. We forget that it is Burbage speaking. The character acquires at once a new dimension of reality. We shall see how this effect of double-bluff is repeated, with more elaboration, when

Hamlet meets a player who can indeed assume the forms and shows of grief.*

[87-128] The King's homily begins as a moral sermon, trite in theme but trenchant in expression, with some telling phrases which give dramatic substance to Hamlet's current behaviour—**to persever In obstinate Condolement . . . unmanly grief . . . A Heart unfortified.** Then he becomes unctuously affectionate—**think of us As of a Father** (the emphasis on his royal pronoun well placed at the end of the line). Then he is publicly magnanimous—**let the world take note**—as he designates the Prince his heir. The crowded playhouse is the world: his public address is to his court, and to us. And when we in the audience (but not Hamlet) are lulled and beguiled by these soft words, suddenly the mailed fist shows for an instant beneath the velvet glove:

> **For your intent**
> **In going back to School in Wittenberg,**
> **It is most retrograde to our desire.**

No sooner shown than withdrawn again, and the speech reverts to flattery and ends with an echo:

> **Our chiefest Courtier Cousin, and our Son.**

The Queen adds her prayers, and unexpectedly Hamlet agrees: the slightest emphasis on the second-person pronoun (**I shall in all my best obey you Madam**) conveys a snubbing disregard of the King's persuasion. At this stage Hamlet's attitude to the King, as Shakespeare suggests it to us, is primarily one of disgust; this unworthy successor has induced his mother to marry him and thus betray the memory of his father. There is no mention made or implied of resentment because of usurpation. The young man would like to renew his student days at the University of Wittenberg: the idea that he must set things right in Denmark is not yet in his thoughts.

The King's relief at Hamlet's unexpected compliance is made plain not only in the exaggeration of the epithets which describe it—**a**

* See *page 70, below.*

loving, and a fair Reply . . . This gentle and unforc'd accord—
but also in the extravagance of his proposal to celebrate it with the
sort of cannonade which is usually reserved for victory in war. We are
to hear this sound of cannon-fire more than once in the course of the
play, and always to good dramatic effect. For the moment, a *Florish*
of trumpets covers the elaborate departure of the state-council.

[129-159] Hamlet lets the procession go by and remains in the
midst of us at the front of the Stage, at the centre of the octagon. He
is alone; we shall therefore expect to see some part of 'that Within,
which passeth show'. The soliloquy was a dramatic convention native
to the Elizabethan playhouse, where the actor stood in the midst of his
audience and in the same neutral daylight; it made possible an un-
selfconsciously direct exposition of motive, situation and character. In
this play the convention reaches its highest degree of complexity and
subtlety; it contributes significantly to the picture of Hamlet who, in
spite of the play-acting forced upon him, is presented to us as fas-
tidiously honest at the centre of the deceiving court; he is surrounded
by enemies and spies, and (but for his exchanges with Horatio) unable
to unburden himself of his inmost thoughts except when he is alone.
The fortunate, but not fortuitous, result of this fact is that we grow
to know his character more intimately (with a more sympathetic
response) than any other in the canon.

The opening groan of this first soliloquy introduces a prelude in
slow tempo, with heavy, reluctant sounds—**solid Flesh . . . Thaw,
and resolve itself . . . the Everlasting . . . Self-slaughter** and the
almost Miltonic weight of **How weary, stale, flat, and unprofitable**
—which expresses his intense self-loathing and disgust with the rank
garden of the world which surrounds him. At first the disgust is
general: no specific cause is identified for us; but the interjections, **O
God . . . Fie on't, ah fie**, predict a quickening of the pace, and from
That it should come to this . . . onwards, the torrent of indignation
becomes more violent and more specific. The framework of Hamlet's
thoughts is **But two months dead . . . and yet within a month . . .
A little Month . . . Why she, even she . . . married with mine
Uncle . . . Within a Month . . . She married . . .**, and the intervening details are not so much digressions as a necessary descant upon that

wicked speed which is finally stigmatised as **to post With such dexterity to Incestuous sheets.** They are moreover the expression of his reluctance; he turns aside, again and again, before he can bring himself to the point of stating explicitly and brutally the cause of his revulsion. And Burbage, suiting the action to the word,* by expressive mime strengthens for us what we feel from this speech of that which is within Hamlet; the nobility of his recollection of his father comes at full stretch of noble stature upon the word **Hyperion**; then **a Satyr** sinks to meanness; a gesture and a change of posture will reinforce the picture of Gertrude's fawning in **she would hang on him**; and his own genuine grief appears in the theatrical pantomime with which he shows how **she followed my poor Father's body Like Niobe, all tears**; a touch of self-deprecating humour adds charm to the contrast of **I to Hercules.** For the rest, the compulsive rhythm, varying like natural speech and growing to a climax like intense feeling, carries the soliloquy to its interrupted cadence. The last line is an abrupt reaction to the sound of intruders: he has promised not to go to Wittenberg: God will not let him kill himself: Denmark is a prison: **. . . break my heart, for I must hold my tongue.** Only when he is alone, only to us his sympathetic audience, can he utter his inmost thoughts. We shall welcome the next opportunity when it comes.

[160-195] The interruption comes from the side of the Stage opposite to where we have seen the King and his court go. At sight of the new-comers, Horatio, Marcellus and Barnardo, we know at once why they have come. There is charm in the contrast between Hamlet's perfunctory response **I am glad to see you well** (spoken before he has turned to see who his visitors are) and the spontaneously affectionate delight of his welcome when immediately afterwards he recognises Horatio. The tone of his three salutations is graded with subtle distinction: Marcellus he knows by name, and he is **very glad to see** him; Barnardo, the sentinel, is politely greeted with **good even Sir.** The Prince who is later described as 'The glass of Fashion, and the mould of Form' has not many opportunities in the course of the play to show the grace and charm which belong to his nature and make him 'Th'

* III.ii.20.

observ'd of all Observers'* and loved by the multitude. Here is one chance which Burbage will take; it is indeed Horatio more than any other who evokes these qualities in Hamlet, and Horatio's dramatic importance in the story is partly just this.

The careful reader may feel that the greeting to Barnardo, **good even Sir**, seems to contradict the promise of the previous scene: the sentries were to bring their news to young Hamlet 'this morning', and we have not been explicitly prepared for a gap of time. But the playwright knows well that the listeners in the playhouse will not notice this inconsistency, if inconsistency it be. At this moment it is necessary that the clock that tells dramatic time should move forward: already we are being pointed towards the night; and when, in a few moments, Hamlet makes his decision to 'watch tonight', we shall feel closer still to the moment of his meeting with the Ghost.

What make you from Wittenberg? asks Hamlet, and he repeats the question, and again: **What is your affair in Elsinore?** Before Horatio can reply—and it is possible to sense some reluctant hesitation in his answer—there is an interruption: outside the Door, where we saw the King departing in high spirits, the sound of revelry jars upon the Prince's mood, and this it is which provokes his bitter comment: **We'll teach you to drink deep, ere you depart.** Bitter too is the sarcasm with which the wicked speed of his mother's wedding is ascribed to the caterer's economy:

> **Thrift, thrift Horatio: the Funeral Bak'd-meats**
> **Did coldly furnish forth the Marriage Tables.**

The words **methinks I see my father** mean that he can guess what his father's reaction would have been, but Horatio, his thoughts full of the news he brings, takes the words literally, and Hamlet's **In my mind's eye** reflects amusement at his friend's obtuseness. Then when Horatio goes on to say **. . . I think I saw him yesternight**, it is Hamlet's turn to be bewildered.

[196-224] Horatio's description of the two appearances of the Ghost before the beginning of the play's action, and of his own sight

* III.i.162, 163.

39

of the apparition, requires great skill of evocation in the speaker. It is part of Shakespeare's method to give extra substance to a scene we have already witnessed in the day-lit theatre by an interpretative description of it after the event:[3] we live again through those nerve-racking watches **In the dead waste and middle of the night**, and we see them now through the 'mind's eye' of the Prince. Incidentally there is material here for the actors who play the Ghost and the watchers on which to base their performance in the earlier scene: we learn here some further detail of the Ghost's demeanour as 'it was about to speak, when the Cock crew':

> **It lifted up its head, and did address**
> **Itself to motion, like as it would speak.**

In the subsequent dialogue we learn too of its pale face, its grizzled beard and its fixed eye.

[225-257] Hamlet's interrogation of the witnesses goes at a brisk speed. The rhythm and variations of pace are written into the dialogue: any attempt to fit the words into a regular pattern of iambic pentameters is purposeless, but it should be noticed that the iambic rhythm continually reasserts itself after extra-metrical interruptions which stem naturally from the excitement of the speakers. At first Hamlet's questions are agitated, and appropriately extra-metrical; but the answers of Horatio preserve as far as possible the metrical regularity of the anxiously sympathetic but positive witness, as if gently resisting the attempt of his questioner to find him out in inconsistency:

> **—Then saw you not his face?**
> **—O yes, my Lord, he wore his Beaver up.**
> **—What, look'd he frowningly?**
> **—A countenance more in sorrow than in anger.**

The brief interruptions of the sentinels add an irregular urgency to the interchange. From the point when Hamlet makes up his mind (**I'll watch tonight**) his words have a cogent rhythmical regularity befitting his resolution to **speak to** the apparition in spite of the dangers of

Hell itself. The indentations of most modern texts show in this passage an orderliness of conversation which is not intended by Shakespeare. Quarto and Folio, as always, print every speech, however short, close to the speech-heading, and allow the calculated balance of regularity and irregularity to sound through the diction of the players.

By Shakespeare's habitual practice, our curiosity is aroused for a scene to come **Upon the Platform 'twixt eleven and twelve.** This we know is 'the platform where we watch'd' in the opening scene of the play. Hamlet's charm is again shown in his parting with them: **Our duty to your Honour** is gracefully corrected by **Your loves, as mine to you.** Left alone, he gives us in short soliloquy his first suspicion of **foul play**: we shall remember this moment when in a later scene he cries 'O my Prophetic soul: mine Uncle?' The curtains of the Study are closed.

*   *   *

[I.iii.1-52]   The intimate sequel is a scene of domestic intimacy, contrasted with the public affairs of the council. The contrast seems at first sight to suggest that this scene is suitably placed above in the Chamber (like the scene between Portia and Nerissa in THE MERCHANT OF VENICE, I.ii, and the sub-plot of KING LEAR, at home with Gloucester and his two sons); but the following scene (I.iv) requires the Chamber for Hamlet's first encounter with the Ghost; and after the explicit promise that Hamlet and his friends will meet 'upon the Platform', Shakespeare would be loth to cheat the audience's expectation by the immediate use of the Chamber for another scene. Laertes's first lines may be taken as one of Shakespeare's characteristically economical indications of locality. Two sailors, bearing some of the **necessaries** of which Laertes speaks—perhaps a sea-chest—and crossing the Stage at the opening of the scene, suggest that the Stage is for the moment the quay-side or the way to it: Polonius says later: 'The wind sits in the shoulder of your sail, And you are stayed for'.

The words and the demeanour of the two speakers establish for us at once the atmosphere of a happy family life: the brother is anxious for the sister's welfare in his projected absence. It is important that we should have this initial impression of a happy and united family: the calamity of Laertes's homecoming is the more poignant. But this scene adds also a further dimension to the portrait of young Hamlet as Shakespeare first presents him to us. After what we have seen of him so far, it will come as a surprise to us to hear that he has been courting Ophelia: but there is no reason to doubt her statement to her father that he has importuned her with love in honourable fashion, and has given countenance to his speech with all the vows of heaven. Laertes's advice to her, expressed at almost hereditary length (his prudence now making an ironical contrast to the turbulence of his later return), is plain enough in intention: Hamlet may love her now, but his love is transient,

> **A Violet in the youth of Primy Nature;**
> **Forward, not permanent; sweet not lasting . . .**

Moreover as heir to the throne, he cannot marry where he will: she should therefore not allow her love for the Prince (evident enough in her whole manner and in the brief eloquence of **No more but so**) to betray her into yielding to his importunity. Q2, by printing inverted commas in front of some of Laertes's lines—

> **'The chariest maid is prodigal enough . . .**
> **'Virtue itself scapes not calumnious strokes**
> **'The canker galls the infants of the spring—**

suggests that he (like father, like son) is given to clinching his precepts with quotations from his commonplace-book. Her innocence is a tender bud (he returns to his image of transience), one of the **Infants of the Spring . . .**

> **And in the Morn and liquid dew of Youth,**
> **Contagious blastments are most imminent.**

In the light of Ophelia's later madness the warning is painfully ironical· Now she acknowledges, with reluctance no doubt, the soundness of his **good Lesson**; and any interpretation of Ophelia's character which denies her innocence is not Shakespeare's. The taste of a later, more indulgent, age should not mislead us. Nevertheless she is not without spirit: she charmingly pricks the bubble of his sermon with her comparison to an ungracious pastor, begging him not to

> **Show me the steep and thorny way to Heaven;**
> **Whilst like a puff'd and reckless Libertine**
> **Himself the Primrose path of dalliance treads.**

Both of them are used to their father's habit of uttering 'precepts',* but their covert smiles during his famous homily are affectionate rather than malicious, and the whole mood is tinged with the sadness of parting.

[53–82] Polonius's urgency on entry—**The wind sits in the shoulder of your sail**—reinforces momentarily the sense of the waiting ship and of Laertes's being **stay'd for**. The reading of the Folio is 'And you are staid for there: my blessing with you'. Q2 has 'And you are stayed for, there my blessing with thee'. If we decide in favour of the Quarto's punctuation, there is eloquent affection in the single word **there**, as Heminges turns abruptly from impatience to a more tender and fatherly farewell. Our earliest impression of the old man is not ludicrous: if we are disposed to smile at him, it is because his precepts have been given before, as is implied in the covert irony of his son's fond comment for his sister's private ear: **A double blessing is a double grace.** His **few Precepts** are neither ridiculous nor unscrupulous; they are good counsel, after the manner of the prudent counsellor, the politic man. In the narrow world of Polonius's conformist morality, the standards are high: Laertes must bear himself gallantly in quarrel, dress as befits his rank, choose his friends well and for life, grappling them to his soul **with hoops of Steel**; but the first approaches should be cautious, he must keep his thoughts to himself, reserve his judgement, remember that his clothes may seem to reflect his character; and he must handle his finances carefully, to preserve both solvency and friendship. This is all the sober advice of a man who knows how to keep his station, but the cadence (**to thine own self be true**) is unmistakably higher wisdom; and Heminges, giving special

* I.iii.58, II.ii.142.

43

force to the words 'thine own self', expresses not only affection but admiration for the boy who has grown up as his father would have had him do. The parting benediction (Laertes properly on one knee) is the more moving in the light of these last lines; Shakespeare has given us the affectionate background against which the private tragedy of the family is to be played.

[83-136] Polonius's line of dismissal has the abruptness of imperfectly mastered emotion: **The time invites you, go, your servants tend.** It seems that the valediction has been made and the scene is over; but at the hint of a secret confidence between the children the old man pricks up his ears, and as Laertes departs for the quay-side, he swiftly pounces on his daughter to satisfy his curiosity.

While Polonius lectures Ophelia, and the focus of interest returns to the theme of Hamlet's courtship, the locality of the scene becomes neutral, and the quay-side is forgotten: this is the method of the unlocalised Stage of the playhouse. Like Laertes, Polonius assumes that it is impossible for the Prince to marry Ophelia: reporting his 'precepts' later to the King and Queen (II.ii.140 ff.), he expresses the position thus: 'Lord Hamlet is a Prince out of thy Star'. In his first dialogue with Ophelia he begins to show those mannerisms of thought and speech which make him later so laughable and yet so true to life— the habit of tortuous and diplomatic digression (**If it be so, as so 'tis put on me; And that in way of caution . . .**); the trick of cracking the wind of a poor phrase, bandying her word **tenders** out of all sense; the occasional sharpness with which he instructs his daughter, the **green Girl**, to carry herself prudently in a deceptive world. If Queen Elizabeth's trusted counsellor, Lord Burghley, was a distant model for the conception of this character, then we have no cause to overlook his fundamental worth: if the part was tailored for John Heminges, 'old stuttering Heminges', we must consider Capulet and Brabantio among his temperamental kinsmen. Polonius's instructions to his daughter are quite explicit: when he has finished circumlocution, he commands her **in plain terms** to have no further communication with Hamlet. Unlike Juliet and Desdemona, Ophelia is prepared to obey.

*　　*　　*

[I.iv.1-38] At once the Chamber-curtains are opened to reveal the battlements of the first scene. The problem before the dramatist (for there was a time when this play did not exist, was still in the process of growth) is to startle us yet a third time with the presence of the Ghost. Q2 (rather than the Folio, according to which the Ghost enters upon the cue 'More honour'd in the breach, than the observance') makes it clear how Shakespeare solved the problem. Marcellus emerges from that side of the Chamber where we remember the sentry-post of I.i: we have been told (I.ii.225) that he holds the watch tonight; so we may deduce that he is pacing his beat when he hears the footsteps of Hamlet and Horatio from the other side of the Chamber. Temperature and atmosphere are rapidly established by poetical means, as they need to be in the day-lit playhouse. Necessity, as so often with Shakespeare, breeds dramatic opportunity: we are told that it has struck twelve, but Horatio did not hear it strike: caught unawares by the passage of time, he is the more acutely aware that the season draws near **Wherein the Spirit held his wont to walk.** Remembering the first scene, we expect this to be the Ghost's cue, and our nerves are on edge, but there is a sudden, almost laughably incongruous, interruption: somewhere from the lower level of the Tiring-House, in the distance from which Hamlet and Horatio have climbed to the battlements, comes the sound of revelry, of trumpets and, from the Huts, of gun-fire. *A florish of trumpets and 2. peeces goes of,* says Q2. Before we have time to recognise Claudius's earlier description of 'the King's Rouse', Hamlet interprets the noise to Horatio in phrases of sarcastic contempt and proceeds to deplore the fact that drunkenness is customary in Denmark and has soiled the country's reputation abroad; the rottenness in the state of Denmark already suggested in I.i is again brought to our attention. This patriotic fervour of the fastidious Prince leads him into philosophical reflection, and he considers the parallel case of the individual whose **one defect** blinds public opinion to his many virtues. Whether or not Burbage's demeanour and intonation suggest that Hamlet is thinking of himself as suffering from the **o'er-growth of some complexion**, the passage seems to reflect Hamlet's role in the tragedy; it is part of the unity of the play. He speaks with compelling earnestness, and we in the audience will be trying to follow the thread of his argument (which, even without the textual problem of the cadence, is difficult); and because we are submerged in Hamlet's absorption, we shall be as startled as the Prince himself at Horatio's urgent warning. For this third appearance of the Ghost, we are not, as on the earlier occasions, carefully prepared: Shakespeare here uses the device of sudden surprise, as the apparition stands in relief against the dark hangings of the Chamber.

[39-57] Hamlet's first instinct is to ask for supernatural protection:

Angels and Ministers of Grace defend us.

For he means to talk with this Ghost: it may come from heaven, it may come from hell, but it looks so like his father that he will risk conversing with it: and his question is (in Doctor Johnson's clear-headed explanation) 'Why dost thou appear, whom we know to be dead?' The difference between paraphrase and text exhibits the extraordinary creative power of Shakespeare's poetic drama. The breathless panic of the opening prayer; the speculation on the Ghost's provenance, presented with antithesis (**airs from Heaven, or blasts from Hell**), and sharpened by chiasmus (**intents wicked or charitable**); the mounting urgency of the separate appeals, each frustrated by silence, and all overflowing into **O answer me**; the retrospective evocation of the scene of his father's burial, with the pathetic resignation of **the Sepulchre Wherein we saw thee quietly inurn'd** jolted by the macabre and startling horror of those **ponderous and Marble jaws,** which have opened **To cast thee up again**; the descriptive interpretation of the present moment, reminding us that this is a **dead Corse** which **in complete steel, Revisits thus** (in the day-lit theatre) **the glimpses of the Moon**; and the final recapitulation of the question **Say, why is this? wherefore? what should we do?**—there are few better examples of Shakespeare's unique power of creating drama through speech, so much meaning is built into this statury group on the upper level of the Globe's Tiring-House.

[58-86] The Ghost's response is to beckon: Q2 has the lapidary direction *Beckins*; the Folio is wordier—*Ghost beckens Hamlet*. And as his habit is, the poet describes and interprets, in the words of Horatio and Marcellus, what we cannot clearly see:

**Look with what courteous action
It wafts you to a more removed ground . . .**

When Horatio, trying to dissuade Hamlet from following, puts his fear into words, his description of **the dreadful Summit of the Cliff** adds greatly to our sense of the dangers of walking by ghost-ridden moonlight on the parapets of Elsinore, and his position in the playhouse, as he looks downward over the rail of the upper level, places him well to put **toys of desperation . . . into every brain That looks so many fathoms to the sea.**

It waves me forth again . . . It waves me still . . . Still am I call'd—before each cue, the Ghost beckons with his courteous action: in effective contrast is the violence of the struggle to restrain Hamlet. The climax of his breaking free is sharply pointed with the wit of **I'll make a Ghost of him that lets me.**

[87-91] Once out of sight, Burbage and the author himself (in full armour) have to scuttle down from above for their next entry. The remaining lines are not, therefore, a mere commenting pendant to the scene; they have their practical purpose, of allowing time for the descent. Moreover they crystallise in a famous phrase—**Something is rotten in the State of Denmark**—that mood of unease which was first hinted at (in I.i) by the sentinel's strange words 'I am sick at heart'; the mood prepares us for the horrible revelations of the Ghost in the next scene. We may imagine that Shakespeare instructed Horatio and Marcellus to take their time over the intervening lines. Horatio is the hesitant one of the two, and Marcellus shows a soldier's impatience of the scholar's inclination to ponder and to leave the issue to the direction of **Heaven.**

*   *   *

[I.v.1-91] The uncanny tension initiated by the sentinels in the opening of the play and so long sustained by the Ghost's portentous silence reaches its climax when he enters through one of the Stage-Doors and shows himself at last at close quarters to the groundlings: the Ghost's courteous beckoning made clear that 'it some impartment did desire' to Hamlet alone (I.iv.59 f.); we know therefore that the time has come for him to speak, and this step forward in the narrative gains immensely from his advance to the middle of the playhouse, to the centre of the Stage close by the Trap-Door (the mouth of 'Hell'). But it is Hamlet who first breaks the silence with his agitated challenge:

Whither wilt thou lead me? speak; I'll go no further.

And in contrast with Hamlet's agitation, in two grave monosyllables the majestical figure commands the attention of both Hamlet and the audience for the long-delayed exposition of the tragedy:

Mark me.

The drama of this meeting of dead father with living son hangs almost wholly upon the spoken word. Of all the tricks of illusion performed in the Globe playhouse, this of the Ghost of Hamlet's father is one of the most remarkable and one of the simplest .With a shock of recollection we remember that Shakespeare himself stood up on the Globe Stage and spoke these lines for the first time. No change of position (we may guess) was necessary, and a bare minimum of gesture, until **the Glow-worm shows the Matin to be near** and, with pathos all the greater for this pitiful meeting, the Ghost once more shrinks in haste away. On the eighty-odd lines of the Ghost's narration depends the whole action of the play. It is for this reason that Shakespeare has written (for himself to speak) verse of such sonority, of such opulent content, such subtle technical detail, such evocative power. Typical but not exceptional is the assonant juxtaposition of **Stars** and **start** where the inverted stress throws eloquent emphasis on the trenchant verb: typical too of the method of the poetic drama is the description of what Hamlet's horror would be, if he knew the secrets of the prison-house, so that at this very moment his hair may be thought to stand on end **like Quills upon the fretful Porpentine.** Hamlet's extra-metrical interjections do not affect the regular pulse of the Ghost's exhortation to revenge: **Murther?** echoes **Murther**, and the triple insistence of this word combines with the iteration of **foul ... unnatural ... foul ... foul ... unnatural** to lend great urgency to the impulse by which Hamlet may sweep to his revenge: and there is contrast in the clogging *adagio* of **the fat weed That roots itself in ease, on Lethe Wharf** (a phrase evocative of the desolate oblivion of the life after death). We take note also of the climactic effect of the deliberate short lines (**And prey on Garbage . . . All my smooth Body**), plain enough in Q2 and not disguised in the lineation of the Folio.[4]

There is pathos as well as majesty in the bearing of the Ghost: Hamlet's first reaction is one of pity (**Alas poor Ghost**), and this compassion reaches its most beautiful expression in the final cadence of 'Rest, rest perturbed Spirit' (*line* 182). The nobility with which Hamlet in his first soliloquy invested the memory of his father is once more evoked in the contrast between Gertrude's two loves:

> **what a falling off was there,**
> **From me, whose love was of that dignity,**
> **That it went hand in hand, even with the Vow**
> **I made to her in Marriage; and to decline**
> **Upon a wretch . . .**

The note of this contrast will be struck again, in the closet-scene (III.iv.53 ff.). The Ghost's final injunction too is characteristic of this nobility:

> **But howsoever thou pursuest this Act,**
> **Taint not thy mind; nor let thy Soul contrive**
> **Against thy Mother aught.**

Such a solicitude appears also with added tenderness in the closet-scene. Nevertheless the Ghost's denunciation of his **most seeming virtuous Queen** is to be marked especially for the effect it must have on Hamlet's already explicit disgust: to her son the hasty marriage itself seemed incestuous; now he is told that there was adultery before her husband's death; and the contrast is poignantly drawn between her husband's love and her lust which was ready to **prey on Garbage**.

Most powerful of all is the unmasking of Claudius, **that incestuous, that adulterate Beast**. The theme of Gertrude's 'falling off' is interrupted as the poor Ghost scents **the Morning's Air**, and he moves with great intensity to his vividly circumstantial account of the poisoning. It is a necessary item in the plot of the play and lends in retrospect great force to the twice repeated re-enactment of the crime by the players of *The Murder of Gonzago*. The repellent physical detail of the description—

> And a most instant Tetter bark'd about,
> Most Lazar-like, with vile and loathsome crust,
> All my smooth Body—

also brings home to us the essential beastliness of Claudius's crime, and its racking effect upon the listening son provides the starting-point for his distraction in the immediate sequel and the hatred which possesses Hamlet throughout the rest of the play. As the Ghost cries out against the crime which robbed him **of Life, of Crown, of Queen**, the language builds in intensity towards the expression of his ultimate misery, in a memorable line of three words only:

> Unhous'led, disappointed, unanel'd.

He died unshriven of his sins. In this way the **sulphurous and tormenting Flames** of which he earlier spoke, the doom he suffers **to walk the night** and **fast in Fires**, the prison-house whose secrets would **harrow up** the soul of his child, all are the direct consequence of the treachery of Claudius. The horror which Shakespeare has here made palpable for us by the verbal method of poetic illusion will have its effect later in the play, when Hamlet ponders on the circumstances of his father's life after death (III.iii.82 ff.).* The story which thus tortures the young man reaches its peak at the triple cry of **horrible**, and it may be that Burbage sank to the ground at the Ghost's feet. Certainly

* See *page 92, below.*

when it has gone, Hamlet is on his knees, calling upon his sinews to 'bear me stiffly up'. That the Ghost, with his fading cry of **Adieu, adieu, adieu, remember me**, descends into the Trap-Door (the 'Hell') is clear from the sequel.

[**92-112**] The distraction of Hamlet's soliloquy is the inevitable consequence of the growing horror of the Ghost's story. As in his first soliloquy, the pattern of both sense and rhythm is cumulative, springing from the Ghost's haunting cadence. He is not, of course, logically or grammatically coherent, but his thought, driven by the urgency of his emotion, grows to resolution. He calls upon the **host of Heaven**; and, kneeling as he is beside the Trap-Door through which the Ghost has just descended, he invokes too with special urgency the **Hell** whose horrors have so recently been pictured for his imagination and ours. **Remember thee?** Yes, I will drive everything else out of my memory (**this distracted Globe**, my brain, **the Table of my Memory . . . the Book and Volume of my Brain**) . . . **yes, yes, by Heaven.** The realisation of the enormity of his mother's crime—indeed no doubt he jumps to the further conclusion that she was party to the murder—confounds him: *line* 105 (**Oh most pernicious woman!**) is incomplete (both in Q2 and the Folio), and represents his inexpressible horror. Then he turns to the thought of his Uncle, and with hammered iterance interprets for us the bland hypocrisy that we have witnessed at the royal council:

> **Oh Villain, Villain, smiling damned Villain! . . .**
> **That one may smile, and smile and be a Villain . . .**

This climax reverts to 'the Table of my Memory'. **My Tables**—no literal note-book here (for what on earth could he be writing in it? his Uncle's name? smiling villain?)[5]—no, he beats his head and commits to it what the poor Ghost has told him: nothing else matters now, no room now for **all pressures past, That youth and observation copied there.** The book of memory is snapped shut with **So Uncle there you are.** The soliloquy comes to a full close with an echo of that poignant farewell and, in a clinching short line, a promise of dedication:

now to my word;
It is Adieu, Adieu, Remember me:
I have sworn't.

[113-149]   The sequel is as astonishing in mood, steering often to the verge of absurdity, as it is theatrically effective. Hamlet's lonely intensity is relieved by the anxious shouts of his companions. They fear for the safety of his soul; when Hamlet hears Horatio's distant cry of **Heavens secure him,** he gives (for our ears only) a feeling reply, **So be it.** The Folio reading, by which Marcellus speaks the words 'So be it', is certainly possible: but Q2, giving the words to Hamlet, provides a more telling moment. As they approach nearer, he answers with a playful imitation of hawking cries. The Stage, after the prolonged static concentration, is suddenly full of rapid movement as Horatio and Marcellus rush about in their nerve-racked quest (reminding us in their mime that it is still dark midnight) and Hamlet for the moment is tempted to play hide-and-seek, dodging round one of the Stage-Posts. The pace of the dialogue is as brisk as the movement of the actors, and the metrical variation most subtly conceived. Sometimes one speaker sustains the metre of his predecessor:

—There needs no Ghost my Lord, come from the Grave,
To tell us this.
—Why right, you are in the right.

Sometimes he ignores it, as Horatio does upon Hamlet's halting half-lines:

—. . . and for mine own poor part,
Look you, I'll go pray.
—These are but wild and whirling words, my Lord.

Sometimes the metrical base momentarily vanishes altogether, as during the excited opening exchange:

—Oh wonderful!
—Good my Lord tell it.
—No you'll reveal it.

Often the resolute resumption of the rhythm is itself eloquent: after the metrical uncertainty of Hamlet's **Yes faith, heartily** and Horatio's **There's no offence my Lord**, Hamlet returns to regularity with his exclamatory retort:

Yes, by Saint Patrick, but there is, Horatio . . .

and continues in his positive assertion of the Ghost's honesty. The rhythm again becomes halting in Horatio's hesitant answer to Hamlet's **poor request**:

What is't my Lord? we will . . .

and the whole exchange grows to a point in a pentameter of deliberate solemnity:

Never make known what you have seen tonight.

Uncertain whom he can trust, or whether he can trust anyone, Hamlet is hysterically excited: he leads his hearers to the brink of discovery, only to change his mind and disappoint them with his levity: **There's ne'er a villain dwelling in all Denmark** suggests the imminent revelation, before it falls into the irresponsible bathos of **But he's an arrant knave.** Horatio's gentle remonstrance, because Hamlet will not confide in him, is touching: but **There's no offence**; he is as selfless as Lear's faithful Kent will be. Hamlet's quick wit fastens on this 'no offence'—**Yes, by Saint Patrick, but there is, Horatio.**[6] But they are not to enquire what the offence is. Charmingly he appeals to his **Friends, Scholars and Soldiers** never to reveal what they have seen tonight. Their honestly ready compliance turns to astonishment at Hamlet's wildly reiterated insistence, **Nay, but swear't . . . Upon my sword . . . Indeed, upon my sword, Indeed**; and so the insistence grows in urgency until the moment when, as if to give eternally binding force to the oath of secrecy, *Ghost cries under the Stage*.

[149-190] This *coup de théâtre* is not the less admirable because it belongs essentially to the theatre rather than to real life. If we pause (but of course we have no leisure to do so) to consider where Hamlet and his companions are supposed to be, we must think of them as somewhere on the battlements of the castle of Elsinore: and in such circumstances, there would be no opportunity for the Ghost to be **in the cellarage** or to **work i'th'earth** like a mole. But Shakespeare's imagination, as always, is composing for his own playhouse: Hamlet and his friends are on the Stage, we have seen the Ghost go down through the Trap-Door, and he is now manoeuvring in 'the Hell' below the Stage, choosing three quite distinct points under which to utter his sepulchral cry of **Swear**. The repeated interruption of the ceremonial oath may cause the audience to laugh, but laughter is often a reflex from other emotions, of awe, of shock, of sorrow; and if the Ghost has wrung our hearts with his address to his son, we shall not feel inclined to mock him underground. Indeed Hamlet's reactions are in themselves an invitation to laughter. Nothing in the scene is wilder than the absurdly joking tone with which he rallies his dead father, welcoming as an accomplice the **truepenny**, the **fellow in the cellarage**, the **old Mole**, the **worthy Pioner**. This frivolity is especially astonishing in juxtaposition to the solemnity of the oath; and especially touching is the effect when Hamlet fastens on Horatio's cry of **. . . this is wondrous strange**:

And therefore as a stranger give it welcome.

What should one do with strangers? welcome them: and his heart is in the word as he thinks of the poor Ghost. And next moment he is gently teasing scholar Horatio with a smile at **your Philosophy**. How many hours of midnight undergraduate argument are conjured up in this affectionately mocking 'your', which we owe to Q2 (the Folio text reads 'our Philosophy').

From the moment of the Ghost's exit to the end of the scene,

Hamlet's behaviour veers between unpredictable extremes—levity and solemnity, savagery and courtesy, irony and pathos: it is a wild and whirling scene: the dominant impression is of hysteria, of the precarious balance of emotions. This hysterical note recurs several times in the course of the play—in the clamorous abuse of the soliloquy in which Hamlet unpacks his heart with curses (II.ii.584 ff.), in the 'nunnery' scene (III.i.124 ff.), in Hamlet's outburst to Horatio immediately after the Mouse-trap Play (III.ii.287 ff.), in the closet-scene, where Polonius is killed and Gertrude's heart is cleft in twain (III.iv), and in the ranting quarrel with Laertes by the grave-side of Ophelia (V.i.288 ff.). When Hamlet in the last scene of the play courteously asks pardon of Laertes (V.ii.240 ff.), his claim that he has been 'punish'd With a sore distraction' is not a mere diplomatic excuse. But this recurrent failure of emotional control is to be distinguished from the deliberate intellectual play of his 'Antic disposition'. Uncritical speculation about whether or not Hamlet is mad is irrelevant. In Burbage's performance we see both instability of temper and counterfeit madness deliberately assumed as a protective cover; it is an unresolved riddle, which adds greatly to the mysterious hold which the central character exercises over the audience.[7]

The passage in which he prepares his friends (and us) for his putting on **an Antic disposition** is a good exercise in the skill of handling the long paragraph. Once again the effect is cumulative, and the framework is **never, so help you mercy . . . this not to do: So grace and mercy at your most need help you: Swear.** The intervening clauses run briskly but are yet (on Burbage's nimble tongue) intelligible, and there is opportunity for mimicry, with variation, in the suggested examples of **some doubtful Phrase.** The Ghost's final interruption caps the rapid injunction with a solemn echo, and Hamlet's **Rest, rest perturbed Spirit** is a quiet consummation to bring the scene to a cadence.

The formal rhyming couplet, expressing the repugnance he feels at the task before him, but also acknowledging his plain duty, to put things right in the state of Denmark, is set, deliberately it seems, in neighbouring contrast to the warm affection of the preceding lines, and the charm of what follows: Horatio and Marcellus are bowing him through the Door, but he says no: **let's go together**, and he gives his arm to his good friends.

* * *

[II.i.1-74] We now have a much-needed relief from the tension of the previous scenes in an episode of domestic comedy. The confined area of the Chamber is a fitting home for this scene, in contrast to the bare Stage which we have come to associate with the dark night of the Ghost's visitation; and we shall see that the long sequel to this short domestic passage requires both Stage and Study for its performance. The Chamber-curtains open therefore and reveal a room in Polonius's house, the old man seated at his writing-table and sealing a letter of instructions to his son in Paris. Q2 tells us: *Enter old Polonius, with his man or two*; the introduction of another member of the household besides **Reynaldo** enables the confidential emissary to add point to his dry comments of stifled impatience by exchanging covert glances of amusement with his fellow-servant. The dialogue is chiefly valuable as developing more elaborately the portrait of the old Councillor and showing, before he becomes centrally involved in the main plot, the habitual cast of his mind—the trick of **encompassment**, of going round about in pursuit of his object, **by indirections** finding **directions out**, and his no less characteristic stubbornness in sticking to his wearisome exposition in spite of his hearer's impatience: he will not tolerate the short-cuts of a quicker intelligence than his own. It is to be noticed that, even in the course of his worldly plan by which **forgeries** are to be laid on Laertes, he makes an emphatic reservation:

> . . . **marry, none so rank**
> **As may dishonour him; take heed of that:**

we are reminded of that regard for his son which we saw in the earlier scene between the two. Especially delightful is the comedy of Reynaldo's inattention, and its effect in compelling Polonius to repeat himself (**And in part him . . .**) before he can recapture the thread of his discourse; and the suggestion of **drabbing, you may go so far,** followed by Reynaldo's protest and Polonius's rejection of the criticism; and the weary interruption of **But my good Lord . . .** and the obstinate old man's quick anticipation: **Wherefore should you do this?** (Wait a moment; don't be impatient; I was coming to that); and the crowning joke of the old man's forgetting his own drift—**By the mass, I was about to say something**—the absurdity well pointed by the collapse from verse into incoherent prose. Once again, the variety and irregularity of the metrical pattern deserve minute study, if the comedy is to be savoured to the full. By the time the impatient Reynaldo has been recalled twice in his attempt to take his leave, we shall be laughing outright.

[74-120] And so we shall be the readier to be startled by Ophelia's abrupt entry from the other side of the Chamber. The boy-player re-enacts for the mind's eye of the audience the episode of Hamlet's irruption into Ophelia's closet, which his author so vividly describes; for it is an important item in the plot of the play. The posture and gesture of Ophelia's mime are dictated by the text; twice during her account an eloquent **thus** implies that her words are embodied in action. The player makes us see the **doublet all unbrac'd**, the hatless head, the **down-gyved** stockings; the grip on her wrist, the retreat to arm's length, the hand over his brow, the attitude of the painter to his model; at last the walk out o' doors without the help of his eyes, and the fixed backward gazing on the frightened girl. In the last line of the speech we feel the finality of Hamlet's farewell to his love with a pathos that defies incredulity:

> **He seem'd to find his way without his eyes,**
> **For out o' doors he went without their help;**
> **And to the last, bended their light on me.**

The episode, properly rendered by a player trained in the method of the poetic drama, will not leave us leisure to suppose that this is the beginning of Hamlet's putting on 'an Antic disposition'. There will be time later for this deliberate and calculated manoeuvre, and its target will be the King and his allies, whose dangerous enmity necessitates such a counter-stratagem. But now, at the moment which poor helpless Ophelia describes, Hamlet is indeed distraught; he wears

> **a look so piteous in purport,**
> **As if he had been loosed out of hell,**
> **To speak of horrors.**

That is, in a sense, just what has happened to him: he has learnt this look from his father, released from his hellish prison-house to tell the tale of that 'most pernicious woman', who had betrayed him; and when we hear that this girl, whom Hamlet has importuned with love in honourable fashion, has lately repelled his letters and refused to see him; when we hear too that he peruses her face **as he would draw it**; we have the first faint hint of a theme which is to be developed later in the play: she too will seem to him as false and fickle as his mother. Frailty, thy name is woman. And all this we shall gather from the animated narration of the boy-player.

Mad for thy Love? Polonius's guess is nearer to the truth than he ever in the sequel comes: for the 'madness' which he later seeks to expound to the King and Queen is partly assumed and partly involuntary: and the frustration of Hamlet's love for Ophelia, soured by his knowledge of his mother's crime, is one cause at least of the 'sore distraction' with which he confesses himself, at the end of the play (V.ii.243 f.), to have been 'punish'd'.

Shakespeare does not intend Polonius to be wholly ludicrous or wholly contemptible: the calamities which befall his household would be less tragic if he were. There is an engaging humility in his confession that his judgement is not infallible, that age can make mistakes as well as youth:

> **By heaven it is as proper to our Age**
> **To cast beyond our selves in our Opinions,**
> **As it is common for the younger sort**
> **To lack discretion.**

Meanwhile we are prepared in anticipation for a visit to the King with a ready-made explanation of the Prince's madness.

* * *

[II.ii.1–39]   And by a simple narrative transition, Hamlet's **transformation** is the immediate theme of the following scene. No sooner have the Chamber-curtains closed on Polonius's house than the Study-curtains open; and there is no need to close them again until the visiting Players want to use the Study space for the preparation of their dumb-show. Hereafter, for nearly thirty pages of the Quarto text, the main action of the play takes place upon the Stage itself: the Study space becomes at one point 'the Lobby' indicated by a gesture as Polonius reminds the King and Queen that Hamlet sometimes walks there 'four hours together': when the King and Queen need their thrones—as, for instance, to receive the ambassadors from Norway, or to sit as spectators of the play—these are brought forward by attendants and placed for them on the Stage and, when not in use, are left inconspicuously beside the neighbouring Doorway: in practice they are probably left so throughout the play, conveniently ignored when (as in the Ghost-scene or the graveyard-scene) their presence is incongruous. But for the time being, until the moment when the story's focus shifts to the Queen's closet, all we need to know is that we are at the court of Denmark—the battle-ground for an absorbing duel between the King and the Prince—and to Hamlet 'Denmark's a Prison', where his actions are spied upon and where eaves-droppers lurk behind the arras.

It has been complained that Rosencrantz and Guildenstern are dull, the biggest bores in the canon. The probable reason for this view is that their personalities seem almost indistinguishable. It is however Shakespeare's plain intention that they should be so: we are meant to notice that when the King expresses his thanks to **Rosencrantz, and gentle Guildenstern**, the Queen graciously restores the balance with a prettily turned echo: **Thanks Guildenstern and gentle Rosencrantz**. This is deliberate and we smile with Shakespeare, not at him. In a later scene (III.ii.54 f.), when Hamlet tells Polonius to 'Bid the Players make haste', he adds—so as to rid himself of the unwanted presence of Rosencrantz and Guildenstern—'Will you two help to hasten them?', and the casual stage-direction of Q2 emphasises the inseparable nature of the pair: *Exeunt they two*. Their part in the plot is essentially that of a pair of collaborators: we have only to consider how much less effective it would be if the King had engaged a single spy to carry out his purpose, to realise how important it is that 'they two' should approach Hamlet in concert, playing up to each other, exchanging covert glances, in the visible act of collusion. Dull they can hardly be, for whenever we see them on the Stage, the duel between Claudius and Hamlet is most keenly engaged, and their attack provokes in Hamlet his most brilliant skill in defence.

Their task is immediately prescribed for them by the King: we hear that they have been sent for in haste, because the King is anxious about what he calls **Hamlet's transformation**, which has changed both the **exterior** and the **inward man**, and which seems to spring from something more than grief at his father's death: they were brought up with Hamlet and their intimacy should make it easy for them to find out if there is something **to us unknown** which troubles him. Full of apparent solicitude, the King would like to find a remedy, if only he knew what the trouble was. They are escorted off by one Door to find their quarry.

[40-58] And from the other Door Polonius enters with the information that the ambassadors, Voltimand and Cornelius, have returned from Norway with good news: and he adds, with habitual circumlocution, that he thinks he has discovered the reason for the Prince's madness. There is a touch of comedy in the councillor's rebuke of the King's excessive eagerness to hear the latter: Polonius is a stickler for propriety, and state matters must come first. It is characteristic of Shakespeare to keep his audience waiting (with a digression which is in itself dramatically important) for an anticipated scene. But the King's preoccupation is made clear to us in his private exchange with his wife; and Gertrude's diagnosis throws a vivid light on her state of mind; knowing nothing of the murder, she is well aware of her son's disgust at **our o'er-hasty Marriage**.

[58-85] Voltimand's report is clear enough in intention, if we have digested the previous accounts of foreign affairs given us by Horatio (I.i.80 ff.) and the King (I.ii.17 ff.). The crisis is over: the reigning King of Norway has checked his nephew's plan to invade Denmark and diverted Fortinbras's ambition to an assault upon Poland: for this purpose he asks Claudius's leave to lead his troops through Danish

territory. Claudius is satisfied with this change of intention, and when in due course (IV.iv) Fortinbras at the head of his army appears upon the Stage, we shall remember his mission and interpret his presence accordingly. The vigorous and resolute ambition of the Norwegian prince is an important strand in the texture of the play. The tapestry is a large composition: but Shakespeare, for all his leisurely weaving, keeps his pattern firmly in mind; and young Fortinbras, introduced to us in the first scene of the play, will hold the centre of the Stage at its conclusion.

[85-159] After Voltimand's twenty lines of static exposition, Polonius rekindles the attention of the audience, giving a lively example of how tediousness can be made entertaining. The subject itself—of Hamlet's transformation—is dramatic enough and the King's eager curiosity and the Queen's brusque impatience, thwarted by Polonius's constitutional inability to **be brief**, make it more so. He begins by addressing them with some formality as they sit on their thrones, but the letter draws them to **gather, and surmise**, one at each elbow. Hamlet's love-letter, written presumably before Ophelia broke off communications with him, and so before there was any suggestion of an antic disposition, is to be taken as a serious attempt in the current Elizabethan fashion:[8] his verses rhyme better than Benedick's, and he is no less apologetic for their quality: Polonius's criticism of the **vile Phrase** 'beautified' is of the same kind as his re-actions to the First Player's performance of the death of Priam; crabbed age and politics cannot live together with artistry and youth. An excellent touch of comedy is the Queen's impatient **Came this from Hamlet to her?** The old man is put out by the anticipation of his climax, and indeed with characteristic obstinacy proceeds with his reading as if the letter's signature were still a dramatic surprise.

The self-righteousness in his account of his dealing with his daughter speaks its own comedy. But it is worth examining the rhythmical vitality which knits together the long paragraphs of this speech. As in Hamlet's first two soliloquies, there is a repeated phrase (varied in shape and position in the line) which impels the forward movement: here **What do you think of me?** is picked up by **But what might you think . . . what might you Or my dear Majesty your Queen**

here, think ... What might you think? The verbatim quotation of his own words to his **young Mistress** is another source of vitality; so is the phrase **and then I prescripts gave her**, which brings a smiling reminiscence of his few precepts to Laertes; indeed the Folio reads 'Precepts' for 'prescripts'; so too is the final protracted catalogue of Hamlet's **declension**, introduced by the promise **a short Tale to make.** Nevertheless, in spite of the element of comedy, it is clear that the King considers Polonius to be **a man, faithful and Honourable,** and that both he and the Queen are ready to place their trust in the old councillor.

[159-170] **How may we try it further?** We do not know at what moment Burbage made his entry. Both Q2 and the Folio (*Enter Hamlet reading on a Booke*) place the direction after the King's line: **We will try it.** Dover Wilson[9] argues persuasively for an earlier entry (at *line* 160) so that a gesture from Polonius—**he walks four hours together, Here in the Lobby**—draws our attention to Hamlet's presence at this very moment: he will then overhear the words **I'll loose my Daughter to him, Be you and I behind an Arras then.** The strongest argument in favour of this interpretation is the explicit bitterness of Hamlet's 'antic' attack upon Polonius in the immediate sequel: he calls him 'Fishmonger' and if this was a well-known slang phrase for 'pandar', the accusation would seem to follow the old man's proposal: 'I'll loose my Daughter to him'. If Hamlet does not overhear these words, Shakespeare has given us no reason in the course of the play hitherto why he should accuse Polonius of being a pandar: so far from loosing his daughter to Hamlet, he has forbidden her to have any communication with him. It is to be observed that the words of Polonius do not incriminate Ophelia as yet. It is only halfway through the 'nunnery' scene that Hamlet's suspicion of her active complicity takes explicit shape ('Are you honest?') and is then put to the test by the question 'Where's your Father?' If, then, we adopt Dover Wilson's suggestion, Burbage is already reading his book at 'Here in the Lobby'. He is in the Study, of course, and, grasping the import of what he hears, he makes a pretence of entering again—for it must not be suspected that he has overheard.

[170-226] The especial interest of Hamlet's first encounter with

Polonius is the depth and variety of mystification which Shakespeare employs. The old man has his *idée fixe* that the Prince is mad for love of Ophelia: even his disordered dress—he appears in the fashion described in such graphic detail by Ophelia to her father (II.i.77 ff.)—suggests the convention of the forsaken lover: Hamlet feeds this obsession by harping on the subject of his daughter, but in such terms that he is puzzled and disturbed—the Prince is mad, but there is **Method** in his madness: although on the surface Hamlet speaks nonsense, on another level his words make sound sense: always in Shakespeare the counterfeit madman, the real madman and the 'allow'd fool' are able in their inconsequential vapourings to reveal truths less clearly apprehended by the sane mind. To those who know the secondary meaning of **Fishmonger** Hamlet's references to Ophelia take the form of a sinister warning. **Let her not walk i'th'Sun**: it would be dangerous for his young daughter to walk in the sun, for it can **breed Maggots** even **in a dead dog**; and woman is frail; why should she be 'a breeder of Sinners' (III.i.125)? And we in the audience do not miss the verbal play of 'sun' and 'son', and the echo of 'I am too much i'th'Sun' (I.ii.67): under the cover of his nonsense does Hamlet speak of himself and of the corrupt world of Denmark in the same breath? We know that Hamlet is in love with her; we have heard (and understood better than Polonius) Ophelia's account of their last meeting. We must be asking ourselves how much of this baiting of her father is the assumption of counterfeit madness and how much the barbed utterance of Hamlet's genuine suspicion. The superficial entertainment of his teasing provokes the audience to ready laughter, but we are constantly jerked back to seriousness and the world-weariness of which we heard in the first soliloquy—**into my Grave . . . except my life, except my life, except my life**. Polonius himself, though he is an easy target, and a figure of fun even when he addresses us *aside* and tells us of his own amorous experiences in youth, is wise enough to appreciate the pregnancy of Hamlet's replies, the madman's felicitous truths **which reason and sanctity could not so prosperously be delivered of** ('sanctity' is the reading of Q2. The Folio, while more rationally reading 'Sanitie', makes a crazy attempt to print the whole speech in verse). Meanwhile the character and attitude of Hamlet become increasingly mysterious, and not only the puzzled old man, but we too, in the audience, even if we sit in the Twopenny Room and pride ourselves on being more percipient, are likewise mystified.

[227-310] Polonius, taking his leave, meets Rosencrantz and Guildenstern in the Doorway. Rosencrantz's **God save you Sir** is his quizzical acknowledgement of the old man's fussily officious indication: **You go to seek the Lord Hamlet; there he is**. Then with a conspiratorial exchange of glances, the pair present themselves. Hamlet's greeting, though not as whole-hearted as his earlier reception of Horatio, is warm enough: the company of his school-mates is welcome in contrast to **these tedious old fools**. The gradual cooling of his warmth is the dramatic interest of the following dialogue. First there is the bawdy back-chat of relaxed student-days; then the first sign of tension (as yet almost imperceptible) as Hamlet questions **more in particular**; the startling pounce of the word **Prison** which, coupled with a melodramatic glance to right and left at the arras-hung Study and Doorways, helps to invest the Stage with the atmosphere of sinister intrigue; then Rosencrantz's feeler about ambition; the perfunctory exercise in logic (another outworn survival of student life), during which first Guildenstern and then Rosencrantz explore, with insinuating iteration, the clue of **Ambition** which seems to be the most significant item in their brief from the King, and Hamlet's weary attempt to break away (**for, by my fay I cannot reason**); the realisation that these two mean to stick to him; the repeated question **What make you at Elsinore?** and the unconvincing reply; the sudden challenge **were you sent for?** and its insistent follow-up: **you were sent for . . . I know the good King and Queen have sent for you . . . be even and direct with me, whether you were sent for or no**; the embarrassment of the pair, vividly interpreted for us in Hamlet's description—**a kind of confession in your looks, which your modesties have not craft enough to colour**—and the desperate question of one to the other (**What say you?**) intercepted by Hamlet with a quick turn of the head; then the final abject confession **My Lord, we were sent for**.[10] The mounting excitement of this detection is supported with all the subtleties of prose rhythm which

Shakespeare has perfected in the duels of Prince Hal and Falstaff
Beatrice and Benedick, Rosalind and Orlando.

[311-329] And nothing is more admirable than the immediate
outcome of this duel of wits. Scarcely disguising his contempt, Hamlet
volunteers to spare them the trouble of telling him why they have been
sent for. He then proceeds to describe for us the melancholy which has
soured the whole of life for him. Embracing with his gestures the
visible **frame** of the playhouse, which shrinks to the **Promontory**
of the Stage, and the *Heavens*, **this most excellent Canopy the Air,
look you, this brave o'er-hanging firmament, this Majestical
Roof, fretted with golden fire,** which he reduces to **a foul and
pestilent congregation of vapours,** he speaks in the imagery of the
Globe, the world of Shakespeare's play. Then pointing his satire at his
former school-mates, he exalts the condition of **a man** to the height
of nobility only to tumble it again to the level of **this Quintessence
of Dust.** It has been well said of this famous passage that 'even as he
voices his own jaundiced view of the reality around him, he affirms
his faith in the wonder of creation and the miracle of man. Hamlet is
sickened by what some men are for the very reason that he is so
acutely aware of what all men should and could be. Only by warping
the lines can we make him a spokesman for modern despair.'[11] His
words rouse wonder and pity in us, who sympathise with him, but
convey no enlightenment to the curiosity of the King's spies: their
subsequent report to their master (III.i.5 ff.), disingenuous as it is, nevertheless confesses the failure of their attempt.

[329-394] The transition which follows this familiar anthology
piece is most ingeniously contrived. Hamlet detects and, in his sus-
picious irritability, mistakes for arch incredulity a smile on the face
of Rosencrantz, who seems to be implying that **Woman** should delight
the mirthless Prince, even if **Man** does not; but Rosencrantz is able,
with some sense of relief, to protest **there was no such stuff in my
thoughts**; he was wondering rather what kind of reception the
strolling players would get, if Hamlet finds no pleasure in the contemplation of his fellow-men; and so the next step in the narrative has
most naturally been made. Hamlet's animated enthusiasm as he hears
of this unexpected arrival is one of those surprising reactions which

continue to sustain the interest of the audience throughout this long and sometimes leisurely role. **He that plays the King shall be welcome** (spoken with emphatic fervour) is a preliminary hint of the importance of this episode in the development of the plot. The topical discussion of the reason for the Players being 'on tour', given at full length in the Folio, but not in Q2, would be more effective in 1601 than in the twentieth century, but though the 'War of the Theatres' and the threat of the Children's Companies to the public stage are no longer common knowledge, there is enough vigour and wit in the phrasing to carry the scene even today, and it is typical of Shakespeare's habit of giving verisimilitude to the circumstances of his story by seeing it through the eyes of his contemporaries: in just such a way the conspirators in JULIUS CAESAR, with their hats plucked about their ears, and half their faces buried in their cloaks, gain added life from their resemblance to their modern counterparts of the Babington plot. Especially interesting is Hamlet's outline of the type-characters of the travelling company—the King, the Knight, the Lover, the Humorous Man, the Clown and the 'Lady'—and the four or five Players who subsequently enter reproduce these types in person. We are skilfully led back from the digression to the main stream of the play. **It is not strange**, says Hamlet: my Uncle's current popularity is just as unnatural as the present eclipse of the Chamberlain's Men by the boys who **carry it away**; indeed, the time is out of joint.

[395-448] The *Flourish for the Players* (an informal improvisation contrasting with the splendour of the royal flourishes we have heard before) quickens the tempo of the scene. Newly vigorous, Hamlet bewilders his companions with the scarce-concealed contempt of his hand-shake and throws in, for good measure, a sardonic warning that he is not as mad as he appears to be: his **Uncle Father and Aunt Mother are deceiv'd.** Then, eccentric still, he makes the pair of them his allies in his game of baiting Polonius. 'Old stuttering Heminges' is the right person to deliver (reading pompously from a play-bill) the parody of playhouse-advertisement, but while we are laughing both with him and at him, we do not miss the serious undertones of Hamlet's seemingly inconsequent interruption:

—O Jephthah Judge of Israel, what a Treasure hadst thou!
—What a Treasure had he, my Lord?
—Why one fair Daughter, and no more,
   The which he loved passing well.

The old man shows a touching sincerity and dignity in the measured tones of his reply:

If you call me Jephthah my Lord, I have a daughter that I love passing well.

We shall be the more distressed for Ophelia later, and for Laertes, because of Heminges's sensitive delivery of this line.

[448-481] The entry of the Players makes a welcome invasion of colour and movement upon the Stage. Perhaps they push a hand-wagon full of their properties and costumes; we have no difficulty in recognising at least the Humorous Man (a sort of Armado-Jaques-Malvolio), the Clown and **my young Lady** (who is of course a boy). Hamlet greets his **good friends** warmly, with badinage for the Player who has grown a beard since their last meeting and for the 'Lady' who has added some inches and is coming dangerously close to the age when his voice will be **crack'd within the ring**. Then he asks for a taste of their quality, **a passionate speech**; and again we seem to drift into a digression, for the play that was **Caviary to the General** had no doubt a topical flavour for Shakespeare's audience that it cannot have now;[12] but again Hamlet's fastidious critical interest in such matters and his particular fancy for **Aeneas' Tale to Dido** add an extra layer of depth to his character; and this episode, like the other digressions, contributes to that rich sense of an external life which is a feature of this play: in the end, though at leisurely length, Shakespeare's dramatic purpose will become clear.

[481-530] The First Player is not a figure of fun nor is his performance absurd: indeed he is very accomplished, in the stylistic convention which is his fashion: this may be that of the neighbouring and rival company, the Admiral's Men, but we may assume that Shakespeare and Burbage were not insensitive to the skill and power of

Edward Alleyn's acting. In any case Hamlet's approval must influence our opinion, and not less convincing as evidence are the reactions of the philistine Polonius and Hamlet's condemnation of them. Hamlet's own recitation of the opening lines of the passage perhaps shows a quizzical exaggeration, relishing the excesses of **Bak'd and impasted** and **coagulate gore**: this is in no way incompatible with admiration for the unknown poet's highly-coloured palette. Polonius's praise is sycophantic (from relief at finding any opportunity to be at one with Hamlet) and it is ignored out of hand: for Hamlet is all agog to hear the sequel. The Player puts all he has into his performance: tone of voice and range of gesture are in the grand manner. Although the episode is a digression from the narrative, it has its place in the play's thematic pattern: the Player's description of **Pyrrhus' pause** before **Aroused Vengeance sets him new a-work** has its direct and ironical application to Hamlet's own condition:

> **So as a painted Tyrant Pyrrhus stood,**
> **And like a Neutral to his will and matter,**
> **Did nothing.**

The last two words stand in rhythmic isolation as a short line in Q2; the metrical hiatus, pointed by a responsive reaction from Burbage, gives us leisure to observe the effect of these words upon Hamlet. He and the other Players follow the story in rapt attention: and we too are witnessing (with the mind's eye) the blow of Pyrrhus's sword and clamouring to the gods against the fickleness of Fortune—when ludicrously, as the Player draws breath for his next line, we hear the voice of old Polonius grumbling: **This is too long.** Hamlet's savage mocking retort, **It shall to th' Barber's, with your beard**, carries all our aesthetic sympathy with it, and we feel no impropriety in the sight of the King's chief councillor being made a laughing-stock among a pack of vagabond actors.

[530-568]   Brushing him aside, Hamlet urges the Player to **Say on; come to Hecuba.** Hecuba was the widowed Queen of Priam. Hamlet's mother is a widowed queen. The poet's epithet 'mobled'—that is, muffled—fascinates Hamlet, and he repeats the phrase, **the mobled**

Queen, savouring it on his tongue, with a reminiscent vision of his mother following his poor father's body 'like Niobe, all tears'. Polonius's attempt to conciliate is both pathetic and comic—**That's good: Mobled Queen is good.** To Hamlet the phrase is not a subject for aesthetic judgement: poor Polonius cannot say the right thing. The narrative of Hecuba's grief is couched in extravagant terms. Indeed the whole passage is loaded with poetical conceits, such as her **threat'ning the flames With Bisson Rheum**, but the remarkable fact is that this inflated style, which Shakespeare has so accurately caught and differentiated from his own style of dramatic verse, can nevertheless draw tears to the eyes of the actor and move his audience likewise. It is clear that Hamlet and the other Players are carried away by the recital: for even Polonius feels the embarrassment of the emotional atmosphere, with his **Pray you no more.** A special interest in this scene lies in the fact that Shakespeare is exhibiting the art of which he himself was a practitioner, the art of acting: that he means his audience to admire what they have seen and heard is plain from Hamlet's injunction to Polonius to treat the actors well, for fear of the power they wield in recording the world they live in: for **after your death, you were better have a bad Epitaph, than their ill report while you live.** Polonius's reply is priggish: **My Lord, I will use them according to their desert.** Hamlet's angry retort reflects his own admirable standard of values, and it is unmistakably sane:

> God's bodykins man, much better. Use every man
> after his desert, and who shall scape whipping?
> Use them after your own Honour and Dignity.

For the moment the antic disposition is forgotten.

[569-583] Hamlet detains the First Player after the rest have followed Polonius: he arranges for a performance **tomorrow night** of **the murder of Gonzago,** with the addition of **some dozen or sixteen lines** of his own composition. The Clown perhaps has imitated the old man's pompous gait behind his back, and this prompts Hamlet's parting shot, **and look you mock him not.** Rosencrantz and Guildenstern, who have watched in baffled silence since the entry of the

Players, are dismissed with the perfunctory repetition of a welcome to Elsinore.

[583-642] Now I am alone. The words make us realise that it is a long time since he was so: Denmark's a prison and his warders have dogged his steps and watched his movements. It has been a long confinement, and the topical digressions and the seemingly irrelevant performance of the First Player have contributed to the impression of length, of delay, of inaction. This has been a part, an important part, of the dramatist's intention. For he wants us to be conscious of the delay, of Hamlet's inaction during this period of stratagem. But it is not the whole: for he wants also to show us that Hamlet is aware of his inaction, that he is impatient of it, and that he is proposing to do something about it. The soliloquy that follows is a bravura exhibition of various moods—ranging from John-a-dreams to the cursing drab— but it ends in resolution and leaves us expecting the first positive move in Hamlet's counter-attack upon his enemy.

Burbage indicates **this Player here** with a gesture towards that part of the Stage where he has given his performance, and re-enacts the details of that performance for us in mime and inflection (the **visage wann'd**, the **tears**, the **distraction in his Aspect**, the **broken voice**), pricking the bubble of his inflated passion with his **all for nothing! For Hecuba!**: this is play-acting, this is a **Fiction** of tragedy; what would he do if his tragedy were real, like mine? And as he drowns the Stage with tears, we inevitably compare the two passionate speeches which Shakespeare has placed in such close neighbourhood. The First Player's speech is deliberately histrionic in its verbal excesses; by contrast, the violent emotion of Hamlet's soliloquy is all the more spontaneous. Shakespeare's bluff is wholly successful: this is Hamlet comparing the Player's pretence with the reality of his own sorrow: we forget that this is the player Burbage pretending to be Hamlet; he is as real as you and I.

In the second phase of the soliloquy Hamlet describes and condemns his own inertia, but in a manner so lively and varied that the actor, using the method of the poetic drama, dazzles us with his virtuosity. First he presents himself as **John-a-dreams**, next moment he represents the challenger insulting the villain, then he once more assumes his own person as the **Pigeon-Liver'd** coward, and from that point works himself up into clamorous abuse of his Uncle, each hammer-blow of repetitive assonance (**bloody, Bawdy villain . . . Treacherous, Lecherous . . .**) aimed at the empty throne at the side of the Stage. Then after the hysterical climax of **Oh Vengeance!** (prominent in the Folio as a separate short line, but omitted in Q2) comes the weary aftermath of disgust at this unpacking of his heart with words.

The reaction from disgust is vigorous planning. We see now why the Players are important, why 'he that plays the King shall be welcome'. They are to play **something like the murder** of the late King before the present King (as he speaks of this, Hamlet outlines the prospective performance in the Study), and if Claudius should **blench**, Hamlet will know what to do. Then at the very end of this self-revelation we are at last given the reason—or at least one important reason—for his hesitation. We do not accept Hamlet's own impatient and over-sensitive interpretation of his delay—that he is infirm of purpose, **unpregnant** of his **cause**—any more than we accept the self-accusation that he is **a Coward**. Now however we hear of a good reason: he is still not certain of the Ghost's intentions. There is no doubt of his hatred for his Uncle, expressed only a moment ago in hysterical rage, or of his determination to exact **Revenge**; but he is no longer under the immediate spell of the majestic form and suffering utterance of the Ghost, and that fastidious honesty which makes him question his own motives leads him once more to uncertainty: the Ghost **may be the Devil**, and in his weak condition of **Melancholy** Hamlet is vulnerable to the Devil's attacks. He must be sure of his Uncle's guilt before he acts: the test will be tomorrow night. **The Play's the thing**—he is standing in the Study as he speaks, gesturing as if the play were already in progress round about him. The finality of the rhyming couplet carries him off, alert and animated with resolution.

*   *   *

[III.i] Critics have complained that this resolution evaporates immediately; that next time we see the Prince he has forgotten his purpose and is contemplating suicide. This surely is not Shakespeare's intention: there is never any question of his abandoning the test of the play to catch the conscience of the King. But after we have been shown

Hamlet's preparation for counter-attack, it is expected that we should see the progress of the King's plans. For this we have been prepared, in Shakespeare's habitual manner, in a previous scene (II.ii.160 ff.). Hamlet, we were told, sometimes walks four hours together here in the lobby: and at such a time Polonius will loose his daughter to him, the King and himself being behind an arras. This projected scene is what we are now to witness.

[1-55] No sooner has Hamlet disappeared than the King and Queen and their entourage come on to the fore-stage from the opposite Doorway: the conversation has begun off-stage, and the King is questioning his spies about the progress of their mission; it is interesting that Claudius describes Hamlet's antic disposition as **turbulent and dangerous**. They can claim little success; in the light of their unhappy interview with Hamlet, and their failure to conceal from him their purpose, it is not surprising that their answers to the King and Queen should be hesitant and general; indeed there is some comedy in their careful support of each other and in the deliberate inversion of truth in Rosencrantz's description of Hamlet's demeanour:

> **Niggard of question, but of our demands**
> **Most free in his reply.**

We remember not only the delicate parrying with which Hamlet kept the spies at bay but also the battery of his questions which elicited their confession.[13] When the Queen asks in maternal solicitude whether they have at least managed to draw him to **any pastime**, Rosencrantz is on safer ground and delighted to answer more particularly. His mention of the visit of the Players pleases Claudius and he accepts Hamlet's invitation (conveyed, it seems, by Polonius) to attend their performance **this night**: a day has passed since Hamlet planned the occasion for 'tomorrow night'—indeed since Hamlet's last exit—but we have no leisure in the theatre to make such calculations or to infer circumstance from them. Rosencrantz and Guildenstern are dismissed, the Queen too invited to withdraw; the trap is baited and Hamlet has been sent for. We notice in passing that the Queen's words to Ophelia (spoken, we may suppose, while the King and

Polonius are preoccupied) encourage her in her love for Hamlet, in spite of her father's instructions. As the Queen goes, Polonius explains to Ophelia her part in the plan: she is to walk about, with her prayer-book to give her a plausible reason for being alone; and he laments in a sententious way the prevalence of hypocrisy. Quite unexpectedly, Claudius, isolated at the very front of the Stage (Polonius meanwhile briefing Ophelia in the lobby; the depth of the Globe Stage inviting the device of the revealing *aside*), betrays to us the **heavy burden** on his conscience. It is evidently part of Shakespeare's plan that, although Hamlet is still uncertain of his Uncle's guilt, the audience should no longer be left in doubt. The scene of the Mouse-trap play gains greatly in tension from the fact that the audience knows not only that Claudius is guilty but that he is already beginning to suffer the pangs of conscience, to see the gulf between his hideous **deed** and his **most painted word**. It is our first opportunity in the play to see beneath the smooth surface of the public figure. After the King's private revelation, he and Polonius slip behind the arras.

[56-88]   Although Hamlet has been 'closely' (that is, secretly) sent for, we shall anticipate his encounter with Ophelia in terms of the original plan of II.ii.160, when we were told that his habit was to walk 'four hours together, Here in the Lobby'. While dramatising Hamlet's long hours of contemplation, is it not likely that Shakespeare will make him carry a book? Indeed, we have seen him doing so already, translating for Polonius's discomfiture a satirist's cruel account of old age (II.ii.201 ff.). The stage-direction in that earlier scene where Polonius first mentioned Hamlet's customary walk is explicit in the Folio text: *Enter Hamlet reading on a Booke.* A repetition of this visual effect here not only reminds the audience of the earlier scene but also of Hamlet's daily routine, on which Polonius relied when he made his plan. Hamlet halts his walk in the lobby and, lifting his eyes from his book, reflectively summarises the contents of the page he is reading: **To be, or not to be**, that's what it amounts to. That is **the question,** the *argumentum* of what he reads. Then he opens the book again, and translates the Latin for a line or two.[14] Then he shuts the book and begins to consider, as students of philosophy will, the nature of death: **to die, to sleep, No more.** (Before this, Ophelia in her walk, seeing

Hamlet so deeply absorbed, has passed from our sight through the Doorway.) This soliloquy, famous in every phrase, was once spoken without the perfunctory utterance of hackneyed familiarity. In the context of the play it is distinctive for its unvarying subdued tone and deliberate rhythm: the sudden emphasis of **Ay, there's the rub**, the flurry of indignation over each of the **Whips and Scorns of time**, the sharp impact of the **bare Bodkin**, the onerous weight of **grunt and sweat**—all these Burbage subordinates to the prevalent minor key and gentle dynamics of the whole passage; and when we reach **the undiscovered Country**, we lapse into a remote depth of contemplation beyond anything we have yet encountered in the play. The trochaic stress of **Puzzles the will** rouses us (still gently) from reveries and prepares us for the philosopher's summary. The contrast of the **Native hue of Resolution** with the **pale cast of Thought** echoes the antithesis of the speech's opening, and epitomises what has already become one of the main motifs of the play. The contrast is not between painful life and restful death, but between patient endurance and positive action; moral considerations argue, perhaps, that it is **Nobler in the mind to suffer**, but to Hamlet such a course seems too close to irresolution, to cowardice; far from being reluctant to act, he is impatient of inaction: his deepest human feelings lead him to prefer the great enterprises which deserve **the name of Action**. In this evil world death may well be a felicity (Hamlet will again think so at the end of his life), but the fear of the hereafter which makes a deliberate escape, by suicide, from an unendurable life impossible, also puzzles the will to act. **Conscience** or cowardice? What is a man to do? We, the audience, are asked not to judge but to understand.

This reflective soliloquy is judiciously placed. For the first time, an objective test of Claudius's guilt seems possible for Hamlet, and he must decide whether or not to follow the instinct which led him to make a vow of vengeance. Later, when circumstances have again forced inaction upon him, he will express to himself, in soliloquy, a similar dilemma, but the application to his own position will be clearer (IV.iv.33 ff.); once again the injunction to patience will seem to him to be the prompting of cowardice (IV.iv.40 ff.). And his decision to act will this time be explicit: 'My thoughts be bloody, or be nothing worth'.[15] But it is to be noticed that the whole of this earlier soliloquy is expressed in general terms; nowhere is there explicit reference to the speaker's own dilemma; in this respect too it is quite different from all his other solo speeches; if what Hamlet here says has a direct bearing upon his personal circumstances, it is left to us in the audience to make the application. At any rate there is nothing in the speech to give us the impression that Hamlet is forgetting his purpose of unmasking the King. On the contrary, Shakespeare has put to good use the necessary interim 'Between the acting of a dreadful thing, And the first motion'.* This soliloquy 'is a meditation on the central theme of the duties and temptations of a noble mind in an evil world, and creates the stillness and intimacy that are needed to prelude his only scene with a girl he once loved, and still loves well enough to wish to keep her unspotted from it'.[16] Meanwhile, it is in a mood of philosophical abstraction that Hamlet becomes aware of Ophelia's presence.

[89-158] He sees that she is at her devotions, and it is quite natural that he should ask her to pray for him too, sinner that he is. There is no irony in his address:

Nymph, in thy Orisons
Be all my sins rememb'red.

For a brief instant we see them as two young lovers, tongue-tied in each other's company. The hideous threatening overtones (his predicament, and hers) do not immediately drown the harmony of their encounter. It is a moment of rare tenderness. But it is only a moment. We have scarcely leisure to think how each could have made the other happy, if only the time were not out of joint. And then she is offering to return the jewels and trinkets he has given her, and he is at once reminded of her inexplicable rejection of his love. It may seem surprising that she, who repelled his letters, should blame him for unkindness: but we must remember Laertes's description (I.iii.5 ff.) of 'Hamlet, and the trifling of his favour', and assume that she has believed her brother's warning; and Hamlet's unaccountable behaviour

* JULIUS CAESAR, II.i.63 f.

in the scene which she described to her father (II.i.77 ff.) can have done little to dispel her acceptance of Laertes's judgement that his love is 'forward, not permanent; sweet not lasting'. Her trite aphorism and the too neat rhyming of **Noble mind** with **unkind** are obvious echoes of her father's instructions. Throughout the early part of this scene between Hamlet and Ophelia the reminiscence of I.iii is unmistakable, not only in that her phrase **their perfume lost** recalls the words of Laertes in I.iii.9, but also in this echo of her father's habit of precept-spinning. This habit and the attitude of brother and sister towards it are carefully and purposefully stressed by Shakespeare in the earlier scene.* To Hamlet however the echo of the old man's moralising is merely laughable: in disgust he proceeds to bewilder her with his riddling wit. She cannot understand him, but we can detect through his whirling words that he talks of his mother, whose beauty has corrupted her chastity, and warns Ophelia against himself in case he should prove a scion of the same tainted **stock** as his mother; indeed the world itself is an unweeded garden. When he first advises her to take refuge in a **Nunnery**, he is giving her serious, though bitter, counsel: 'if you and I married, our children would be sinners; for look at me; I am more or less chaste, but I am so full of sins that it would have been better if my mother had not borne me: enclose yourself from a corrupt world.' The speech ends with, it seems, a farewell injunction, **We are arrant Knaves all, believe none of us. Go thy ways to a Nunnery**, and he turns to leave her; but then follows an abrupt and startlingly inconsequential question, **Where's your Father?** Clearly his suspicions have been roused, perhaps by the mere sight of the arras in the Doorway, as he turned to leave. The reader is referred to Coghill's excellent analysis of this scene.[17] He is certainly right in suggesting that there is no need for a clumsy movement of betrayal by Polonius or the King, hidden behind the arras; right too that this is the moment when Hamlet's suspicions are aroused. Although he and Dover Wilson differ in their readings of this particular scene, Coghill's interpretation is compatible with Dover Wilson's theory that in II.ii. 162 ff. Hamlet overhears Polonius's plan to use Ophelia as a decoy. He feels that Ophelia is potentially a danger, even unconsciously allied

* See *pages* 42, 43, *above*.

with his enemies; so the sins which he claims for himself are deliberately chosen (is it a felicitous coincidence that in the Folio text only one of Hamlet's self-accusations is awarded the status of a capital letter?):

**I am very proud, revengeful, Ambitious, with
more offences at my beck . . .**

He suspects that he will be reported. But it is at the moment when he turns to go and his eye falls upon the arras, that he remembers the exact circumstances of the plot, and suspects that their conversation is overheard. **Where's your Father?** is his crucial test of her.

We cannot be certain how Shakespeare instructed the boy-player to render Ophelia's line **At home, my Lord.** At least two interpretations are possible. It is usually supposed that she is telling a panic-stricken lie, to cloak her father's deception; but perhaps we are meant to think that she is speaking what she believes to be the truth, and is simply bewildered by Hamlet's explosive reaction. The latter view involves our supposing that in III.i.28–49 Ophelia is standing at a respectful distance out of earshot of the private counsels of her father and the King (a disposition of grouping which is as easily attained as it is habitual upon the Globe Stage with its resources of depth and breadth); and that when (at *lines* 188 f.) Polonius says 'You need not tell us, what Lord Hamlet said, We heard it all', he is telling her (what she has not hitherto known) that he and the King have been eavesdropping.

Hamlet at any rate takes her answer to be a lie, and it provokes the explosion, and his violent railing convinces her that he is mad indeed. We know of course that he is not mad—not in the sense that Lear on the heath is mad, or later in this play poor Ophelia herself, out of her wits. We see again the hysteria that overtook him in I.v;* and so his cry of **it hath made me mad** is not altogether play-acting. On the other hand, he has logical cause for his distraction: she has now proved herself, to his eyes, as wanton as his mother, and as all the rest of womankind. The iteration of his cry **to a Nunnery** sustains the rhythm of his

* See *page 55, above.*

invective (and it is likely that Burbage's audience took the point, as we cannot, of the quibble which identified 'nunnery' and 'brothel'; what began as serious advice becomes, by word-play, a cruel attack). The parting shot of **those that are married already, all but one shall live** is directed at his Uncle behind the arras. And he is gone— and Ophelia's romance is in ruins.

[159-170] Left alone for a moment, while the unseen watchers assure themselves that the coast is clear, she utters her little poem of lament. It is a poem, with a formality of pattern and balanced phrases which defies realistic delivery. Shakespeare will sometimes adopt such formality in the expression of deep feeling, and it may be that he found it more suitable to the talents of his boy-actors, who would not have been allowed to slur or disguise the shape of such a line (expressively emphasised by the Folio's colon, which modern usage would reject as syntactically irregular) as **The Courtier's, Soldier's, Scholar's: Eye, tongue, sword.** The static style of utterance makes a deliberate contrast with the dynamic energy of what precedes it. We have leisure to contemplate the promise of Hamlet's youth (not hitherto revealed in the dialogue of the play) and the declension which has blasted it. The distinction is summed up in her pathetic cadence—what she has seen in days gone by, and what she sees now.

[171-197] The King, with characteristic determination, declares his diagnosis: Hamlet is not in love, and he is not mad; he is dangerous; he must therefore be sent on a diplomatic mission **to England**; the change of air may cure him. Polonius, obstinate as is his habit, sticks to his belief that Hamlet's trouble is his rejection by Ophelia. The brusqueness of her father's words, seemingly unaware of her distress, will always raise a wry smile in the audience; instantly extinguished, as we note the incredulous horror on the girl's face at her father's lack of understanding. A parallel is Juliet's horror at the cynical 'comfort' given by her Nurse (ROMEO AND JULIET, III.v.214 ff.), but in that scene the horror is given explicit expression after the Nurse's departure. Polonius has an alternative plan to suggest to the King: after the play, let his mother **be round with him**, and I will listen behind the arras again: if that produces nothing, send him to England. So now we have three developments to look forward to—the play, the meeting between mother and son, and the voyage to England. It is Shakespeare's habit to excite our curiosity for the future.

*   *   *

[III.ii.1-56] The continuity of the play is unbroken, for our interest is in suspense, anticipating the performance of 'The Murder of Gonzago'. Now it seems at first sight that our expectation is to be fulfilled immediately. On the departure of the King and Polonius, the curtains of the Study remain open. One or two of the Players begin busily placing in the inset space the crude furniture needed for their play—a back-cloth suggesting a garden, a property 'moss-bank' for their 'King' to sleep on, and perhaps a property tree to shade his slumbers. They are half-dressed for their parts, the boy (in his farthingale as Queen but without his wig) engaged in most unqueenly manual exertion. Claudius's last words ('Madness in great Ones, must not unwatch'd go') are still sounding in our ears when Hamlet returns to join the Players. As they gather round him to listen to his advice, he once again astonishes us with a change of mood: so far from madness, he is unmistakably sane. By this means, a time-gap is subtly suggested without breaking the continuity of the play's movement.

The transition in plot is swiftly made in Hamlet's first sentence: he is discussing that 'speech of some dozen or sixteen lines' which he himself proposed to 'set down, and insert' in the Players' script. The stir and bustle for the command-performance will take time, and once again (our expectation of immediate action whetted) Shakespeare allows himself a leisurely digression, making Hamlet lecture his actors on the subject of their craft; another strand in the character of this fastidious and cultivated Prince is revealed to us. His strictures are of course not aimed at the Chamberlain's Men (who would hardly have relished putting themselves in the pillory) but rather at the excesses and absurdities of the rival companies. Hamlet has already expressed his views about what makes 'an excellent play . . . set down with as much modesty, as cunning'. Now he attacks extravagance not only of writing but also of performance:[18] and the acting-style of the Mouse-trap play may have contained some touches of caricature in recognisable imitation of individual members of the Admiral's company.

But we should notice that, while actors of all generations receive from a practitioner of their art advice which they cannot afford to ignore, the audience too are treated to some instruction from their favourite poet: Burbage gives the **Groundlings**, standing at his elbow, the rough edge of his tongue, rallies the **unskilful** for their unsympathetic laughter, and tilts at **some quantity of barren Spectators**, while at the same time paying a tactful compliment to **the Judicious**, whose individual opinion is more important to actor and author than all the rest of the audience put together. Shakespeare, both in this passage and in the previous dialogue about the theatre (II.ii.348–565), shows his confidence in the esteem which he and the Chamberlain's Men have won for themselves as the leading theatrical company in London, and claims for the art of the drama a new dignity and importance. The fooling of the Clown, who is at this moment diverting the attention of some of the groundlings from Hamlet's lecture, makes him an easy butt for the sharp cadence, **that's Villainous, and shows a most pitiful Ambition in the Fool that uses it**: the joke is turned against the joker. **Go make you ready** is a cue for the closing of the Study curtains. Polonius, announcing the imminent arrival of the King and Queen, withdraws again immediately to escort them in; and Rosencrantz and Guildenstern are summarily dispatched within the curtains to help hasten the Players. *Exeunt they two.*

[57–94] And again Shakespeare surprises us, with an unexpected change of subject—as he so well knows how to do, when our curiosity is all agog for the excitement of the sequel. Here follows a quiet passage of heart-felt intimacy in which Hamlet confesses how much Horatio's friendship has meant to him: it is expressed with the utmost delicacy, with eloquent hints (in Horatio's modest **O my dear Lord**, and Hamlet's **Nay, do not think I flatter**; and again in the half-embarrassed withdrawal of **Something too much of this**): and it prepares us for the last Act of the play, giving us a much profounder understanding of Horatio's constant sympathetic attendance on Hamlet in the grave-yard scene and thereafter. Hamlet, in thus paying tribute to Horatio, reveals also something of his affectionate self; in this narrative of revenge such moments are rare enough, and this one is carefully placed just before the savageries of the following scenes.

Horatio, **as one in suffering all, that suffers nothing**, has that equanimity which Hamlet, **Passion's Slave**, finds lacking in himself. That is why he wears him in his **Heart of heart** (a phrase as full of meaning, on the analogy of 'heart of oak', as the cliché 'heart of hearts' is vapid). Turning abruptly from this mood, he explains to Horatio (and to us) the exact details of his plan to catch the conscience of the King. **One speech** is the crux—the speech which he himself has inserted in the text—and if the King does not give himself away, the Ghost is sent by the Devil, and Hamlet's suspicions are the morbid result of melancholia. Watch him, and **I mine eyes will rivet to his Face**. It is significant that Horatio, now in Hamlet's confidence, makes no objection to this reasoning. His laconic acquiescence indicates that he too believes this test of the King's guilt is at the same time a trial of the Ghost's honesty.

[95-146] This private conversation is interrupted by the sounds of music proclaiming the arrival of the audience to see the play: Q2 asks for *Trumpets and Kettle Drummes*, reflecting Hamlet's description of the King's 'rouse' (I.iv.11): the Folio specifies a *Danish March* (perhaps the stage practice at this point had been changed to suit the growing interest in Denmark under King James). It is the first public occasion for many pages of the text, and the Stage fills with animation and colour. The *Torches* of the Folio's stage-direction increase the sudden splendour of the scene. The Study (with curtains at present closed) being reserved for the performance of the Players, the thrones for the King and Queen are brought forward beside one of the Stage-Posts. The King halts in mid-stage to greet Hamlet, who before our eyes has assumed his antic disposition (**I must be idle**): then stiffly rebuking his nephew's quibbling mockery, he joins Gertrude already seated on her throne. Polonius, pompously affable, is made the butt of outrageous punning. This sharp word-play was peculiarly apt at the Globe, if Baldwin is right in suggesting that Heminges played Caesar before he played Polonius: but the exchange of words with Hamlet not only raises prompt laughter in the playhouse; it also adds a further touch of verisimilitude to the rounded portrait of the Councillor:

—My Lord, you play'd once i'th'University, you say?
—That I did my Lord, and was accounted a good Actor.
—And what did you enact?
—I did enact Julius Caesar, I was kill'd i'th' Capitol:
   Brutus kill'd me.
—It was a brute part of him, to kill so Capital a Calf there.

Unabashed, Polonius goes to stand close beside the King, so that he may whisper his comments in his ear. Rosencrantz comes through the Study-curtains to tell us that the play is ready. Hamlet, insultingly ignoring his mother's invitation, squats on the ground at Ophelia's feet, as she sits beside the other Stage-Post. Horatio close behind them is a conspicuous watcher.

Hamlet's cruel baiting of Ophelia, publicly treating her as if she were wanton, follows the vein of his tirade of the previous scene: and her dignified reticence cannot cancel our recent memory of her distress: when next we see her, she will be out of her wits. But the bitter irony of **die two months ago, and not forgotten yet?** is aimed at his mother, whose cheerful looks, as she chatters with Polonius, reflect her unsuspecting relief that her son takes pleasure in the delights of play-acting.

[147-286] This court performance has its own musical introduction. Q2 has *The Trumpets sounds*, reminding us perhaps of the flourish which presaged the appearance of the Players in II.ii. The Folio directs that *Hoboyes play*, which suggests more appropriately chamber instruments contrasting with the elaborate music of the royal entry. The Study-curtains open, and the *Dumbe Show followes*. The players, following traditional practice, enact in mime a brief summary of the story they are about to present. (A similar preliminary dumb-show accompanies Quince's introduction to 'Pyramus and Thisbe' in A MIDSUMMER NIGHT'S DREAM, V.i.129 ff.) Everybody watches[19]—the courtiers with casual amusement, for they see no obvious relevance to reality; Gertrude uneasy and embarrassed at the behaviour of the 'Queen', but merely puzzled at the scene of the poisoning; Claudius gradually more and more aware of a sinister purpose in the choice of the play, and shying away from the eyes which Hamlet rivets on his

Uncle's face. Hamlet's audible *asides* to Ophelia (**it means mischief,** the Players will **tell all**) announce the trap which he has laid to catch the conscience of the King. Murder by poison was Claudius's solitary secret; yet now it seems that Hamlet too knows the truth. Shakespeare has prepared us to watch the prolonged ordeal which is to test the murderer's nerve, and the deliberate pace of the subsequent formal dialogue gives us leisure to enjoy each phase of Claudius's discomfiture; after the Dumb Show both Claudius and the audience know precisely the point at which the climax of the Mouse-trap play will occur, and the tension grows steadily.

If Claudius were not already alerted to his danger, the length and slow pace of the dialogue between 'King' and 'Queen' would be tedious and undramatic. It hardly needs seventy lines to establish the point that a wife's vows of fidelity to her husband may be forgotten after his death. But the flat formal couplets are perfectly conceived as a background to the tense drama we witness on the fore-stage; and the rhymes have an epigrammatic force which gives point to the salient themes. Having put his Uncle on the rack, Hamlet turns his attention during the first part of the play to his mother, and on the 'Queen's' couplet,

> **In second Husband let me be accurs'd,**
> **None wed the second, but who kill'd the first . . .**

his comment of **Wormwood, Wormwood** shows us that he believes her to have been an accomplice in the murder. **If she should break it now** is aimed straight at his mother, and on the 'Queen's' exit, he rises from his seat by Ophelia and crosses over to ask **Madam, how like you this Play?** Her brave attempt to brazen it out is silenced by the calculated insult of **Oh but she'll keep her word.**

And then Claudius joins issue, and we think for a moment that he will summarily put an end to the proceedings, if there is to be some offence in the play. **No, no, they do but jest, poison in jest** (of course Claudius has seen the poisoning in the Dumb Show), **no Offence i'th'world.** And there is great relish in Hamlet's mounting excitement as his enemy falters:

> **The Mouse-trap . . . 'tis a knavish piece of work:**
> **But what o'that? Your Majesty, and we that have free**
> **souls, it touches us not . . .**

Then he crosses back to Ophelia, announcing the entry of the villain, **one Lucianus nephew to the King** (might not a King's nephew murder his uncle?). While Lucianus goes through the motions of a melodramatic villain, making his **damnable Faces,**[20] poor Ophelia tries to parry some more brutalities of speech from her sometime lover, and then Hamlet's excitement bursts all bounds and he calls upon the Murderer to speak the 'dozen or sixteen lines' which he himself has written for the climax of the play. The speech is but half-way through, and the Murderer is bending over the sleeping figure of the 'King' (the Folio has the explicit direction: *Powres the poyson in his eares*), when Claudius's nerve snaps, and Hamlet, not meaning to forgo the moment of his triumph, shouts the rest of the story full in his Uncle's face:

> **He poisons him i'th'Garden for's estate . . .**
> **You shall see anon how the Murtherer gets the love of**
> **Gonzago's wife.**

After the tense concentration upon the Players' performance, the sudden collapse into general confusion is a brilliant stroke of theatre. The King rises from his throne and staggers across the Stage, clamouring for **some Light** to conduct him through the dark corridors of the palace; we see the gathering of more torches in the Doorway; Polonius bustles over to the Study to dismiss the startled Players from their stage (**Give o'er the Play**), and in bewilderment they begin to dismantle their property tree and *Banke of Flowers*; the courtiers follow the King, Rosencrantz and Guildenstern being especially officious in their duty; evidently the general impression is that the Prince in his madness has made a treasonable attack upon their sovereign; the 'nephew to the King' is planning murder. The swirl of colours and light and the rapid disorderly movements make a dramatic climax of great power, and as the Stage empties, and the Study-curtains close, the confusion of frightened cries and angry shouts merges into a single hysterical outburst of laughter. For Hamlet, with his ever faithful Horatio, is left in possession of the field of battle.

[287-307] Hamlet's excitement in the following passage reminds us of his mood while telling Horatio and Marcellus of his conversation with the Ghost;* but then he was keyed up by the horror of the Ghost's revelations, whilst now he is exhilarated by his momentary triumph over his enemies; and in his treatment of Rosencrantz and Guildenstern, and later of Polonius, he takes confident advantage of their discomfiture. His first reaction is to break into doggerel verse, probably transparent parody of popular ballads of Shakespeare's time, and to congratulate himself in exuberant imagination on his skill as a playwright, earning him a share in the Players' company (Shakespeare himself had a share in the profits of the Chamberlain's Men).

> **For thou dost know Oh Damon dear**
> **This Realm dismantled was**
> **Of Jove himself, and now reigns here**
> **A very very pajock.**

His father was **Jove**; the sinister, lustful peacock is his Uncle. Horatio (his **Damon**), not being passion's slave, is more temperate in his agreement, but he too is in no doubt that **the Ghost's word** is to be trusted: for Claudius blenched **upon the talk of the poisoning**. In exultation Hamlet calls for **some Music** to celebrate the King's defeat.

[307-396] Rosencrantz and Guildenstern have come hurriedly back, with an urgent message from the Queen. In Q2 they enter after the second call for music. In the Folio they enter upon the cue **I did very well note him.** The latter text suggests that **Oh, ha?** is a recognition of the spies' presence; that the call for music is a diversion to confuse them; and that Hamlet deliberately taunts them with his jingle:

> **For if the King like not the Comedy,**
> **Why then belike he likes it not perdy.**

* See *page 55, above.*

85

Still jubilant from the success of his plan, he puts on his antic disposition once again, and revels in exercising his ironic wit upon the pair of them. They are now less obsequious, a little firmer, in their handling of the 'madman', but they are not a match for his contemptuous parrying of their attack. Mocking them with deliberate misunderstanding, when he is asked to give **a wholesome answer**, he says **I cannot . . . my wit's diseas'd**. We in the audience, having shared the privacy of his soliloquies and of his friendship with Horatio, are able to appreciate the irony of his pretended madness; and when Rosencrantz delivers his message, that the Queen **desires to speak with you in her Closet, ere you go to bed**, the intense earnestness of his reply, **We shall obey, were she ten times our Mother**, is not lost on us.

Undeterred, Rosencrantz tries once again to elicit from Hamlet the **cause** of his **distemper**, this time by an overt appeal to the affection which, we have heard, the Prince once felt for his friends:

My Lord, you once did love me.

But Hamlet coldly fobs him off again with the hint, now more explicit and menacing, of frustrated ambition:

—Sir I lack Advancement.
—How can that be, when you have the voice of the King himself, for your Succession in Denmark?
—Ay, but while the grass grows . . .

Then as one of the Players returns through the Study-curtains with his instrument, answering the call for music, Hamlet seizes the pipe from his hands and makes a parable out of it for the embarrassment of Guildenstern: he begs him to play: and when the helpless courtier protests his inability, Hamlet torments him with pressing repetition of his ironically polite request:

—My Lord, I cannot.
—I pray you.
—Believe me, I cannot.
—I do beseech you.
—I know no touch of it, my Lord.

Suddenly there is a sharpening of Hamlet's tone: **'Tis as easy as
lying**. And when Guildenstern continues to plead that he has not **the
skill**, there comes in accusing anger the application of the parable:
you would play upon me. The comparison of himself to a pipe
produces a beautifully measured sentence of intimate self-expression
reminiscent of the inwardness of his earlier revelation: 'I have of late,
but wherefore I know not, lost all my mirth . . .' (II.ii.313 ff.). Now
as he says **you would pluck out the heart of my Mystery**, he is
speaking in the same vein, and Burbage joins together his performance
over a long span of the play by recalling the tone of his very first
scene in the words 'I have that Within, which passeth show' (I.ii.85).
But the abrupt exclamation **'sblood do you think I am easier to
be play'd on than a pipe?** and the sharpening of his thrust with
characteristic word-play (**though you can fret me, you cannot play
upon me**) jolt us—and Guildenstern—out of the introspective mood
and bring us to the trenchant end of the angry parable.

[397-412] With the entry of Polonius to reinforce his mother's
command, Hamlet develops the antic disposition to the height of
absurdity. It becomes a test of sycophancy: the old man humours the
madman with elaborately patient acquiescence: **yonder cloud is like
a Camel indeed . . . back'd like a Weasel . . . Very like a Whale.**
His sidelong glances exchanged with the two courtiers suggest that the
joke is at Hamlet's expense: but we in the audience, who have shared
Hamlet's confidence in soliloquy, can relish the irony of Polonius's
obtuseness. Hamlet's irritable comment (**They fool me to the top
of my bent**) is thrown *aside* over his shoulder to Horatio. Polonius
goes back to report Hamlet's coming **by and by**: Rosencrantz and
Guildenstern are dismissed in the same direction—for presumably
they go to find the King—with an ironical **Leave me, Friends**: and

Horatio, with no need of bidding, retires by the opposite Door. Once more Hamlet is alone.

[413-424] In four or five lines of poetic evocation Shakespeare transforms the atmosphere of the playhouse to sinister midnight:

> **'Tis now the very witching time of night,**
> **When Churchyards yawn, and Hell itself breathes out**
> **Contagion to this world ...**

Even so, in a later play, Macbeth brings down the grim twilight to prepare us for the murder of Banquo. Then Hamlet reminds us of the Ghost's injunction—'nor let thy Soul contrive Against thy Mother aught'—and in his parting cadence promises cruel words but not unnatural deeds in the coming interview with his mother. He goes out (following the logic of the story) by the same Door as Polonius on his way to the Queen's closet.

*　　　*　　　*

[III.iii]   This is a phase of the play in which Shakespeare is at pains to give us some precise localisation: from the hall of the palace in which the Mouse-trap play took place Hamlet passes through the chapel or private chamber of the King and on to his mother's closet; after the killing of Polonius the journey is reversed: pursued by his warders, Hamlet returns—via the now off-stage lobby next to Gertrude's closet, where he has disposed of the body, lugging the guts into 'the Neighbour room' (III.iv.212)—down the stairs until he is caught and arraigned before the King; then comes the callous direction to the seekers 'you shall nose him as you go *up the stairs* into the Lobby' (IV.iii.39 f.). The use of both levels of the Tiring-House and Stage is helpful in the tracing of this pattern.

We cannot be certain about the 'plotting' of these scenes, since the ways in which the playhouse areas were used are a matter of dispute. Nevertheless it is possible to work out a disposition by which the structure of the playhouse will seem to be of great importance in illuminating the shape of the narrative. The last part of III.ii (after the

Mouse-trap play) takes place on the main Stage, with the Study-curtains closed. Let us assume, as a starting-point from which to deduce the pattern, that Hamlet leaves by the Right Door. The Study-curtains open to reveal the King's chapel; in due course Hamlet, as if ascending in a spiral, enters by the Left Door and runs round the perimeter of the main Stage on his way to his mother's closet. At the end of the scene, continuing the logic of his direction, he leaves by the Right Door. The Study-curtains close on Claudius, and the Chamber-curtains open to reveal Gertrude's closet, distinctively upstairs. Both Polonius and Hamlet (by the logic of the story) enter the closet from the Left-hand side. At the end of the closet-scene Hamlet lugs the guts away towards the Left and, after hiding Polonius and running down-stairs, he will reappear with the words 'Safely stowed' (IV.ii.1) by the Right Door on to the main Stage.

[1-26] We have never, in the course of the play, seen Hamlet and his mother alone together, and in our eager expectation of this critical meeting, we shall not foresee the immediate sequel. But it is Shakespeare's habit to turn aside to other material while he knows that our curiosity is aroused and our interest held in anticipation. The curtains of the Study, which have been closed since the interruption of the 'play', open again at this point and reveal furniture which suggests a private chamber or chapel in the palace. No more is needed than a prie-dieu and fald-stool, with a crucifix suspended before them, set at such an angle that the penitent prays towards one side of the Study, with his back to the other side of the Stage.

The King and his minions enter within the Study-space. He is in a state of agitation, as is natural after his last departure. But he is also characteristically resolute, and the previously conceived plan of sending the **dangerous** madman **to England** is to be put into immediate execution: Rosencrantz and Guildenstern are to be his escort. Their attitude to the present crisis, expressed at some length, is not to be ignored or slurred over. Their language is sycophantic:

> **Most holy and Religious fear it is**
> **To keep those many many bodies safe**
> **That live and feed upon your Majesty.**

But their view is in no way foolish. Hamlet threatens the life of the King; upon the King's safety depends the prosperity of the whole realm:

> **the cease of Majesty**
> **Dies not alone; but like a Gulf doth draw**
> **What's near it, with it.**

This is the orthodox and conventional attitude, and even in the last moments of the play, when Hamlet wounds the King, the action provokes a general cry of 'Treason'. Hamlet's situation throughout the play is thus seen to be the more difficult and dangerous, if it is realised that he is virtually alone, pitting his wits against the whole body of court opinion. And Shakespeare's audience (as the author of RICHARD II, JULIUS CAESAR and MACBETH well knew) was much exercised by the subject of tyrannicide. Elizabeth and James I were both exposed to the danger of assassination; and across the water, in France, the ethical problem of removing an unacceptable monarch was still more acute and more explicitly discussed.[21]

[27-35] Rosencrantz and Guildenstern hurry off, and at once Polonius appears: he warns the King that Hamlet is on his way to his mother's closet, and reminds us of his own intention to lurk 'in the ear Of all their Conference'. Even at this critical moment, the old man indulges in his habit of digression, qualifying his clauses (**And as you said, and wisely was it said . . .**). We can sense the premonitory irony of his promise: **I'll call upon you ere you go to bed.** The Doorway by which he leaves the Stage is established as the way to the Queen's apartment.

[36-72] Left alone, the King approaches the prie-dieu, but he does not attempt to pray until the end of his soliloquy. This exhibition of the criminal, wavering between hope and despair (**Oh limed soul, that struggling to be free, Art more engag'd**), is most powerfully moving. What makes Claudius an especially interesting figure among Shakespeare's villains is the activity of his conscience, which so unexpectedly underlies the unscrupulous ruthlessness of his statesmanship: we have already had a hint of this in that impromptu reaction (spoken *aside*) to Polonius's moralising (III.i.49 ff.). First there is the

downright statement of the crime—**Oh my offence is rank . . .**—and we remember Hamlet's hatred of the unweeded garden of the world possessed by 'Things rank, and gross in Nature'. Claudius stigmatises his own crime with the **primal eldest curse** of Cain; and after the statement of **A Brother's murder,** there is a momentary pause (for both in Q2 and in the Folio the line is short of one stressed syllable); and then **Pray can I not.** Now his intent to pray is strong, but his guilt is stronger: prayer can forestall sin, or win pardon for sin when already committed: **Then I'll look up.** But how can he pray for forgiveness and still cling to the rewards of his crime, **My Crown, mine own Ambition, and my Queen . . .** ? You may dodge justice in this world, **but 'tis not so above, There is no shuffling** (the poet's sense depends upon the player's speaking: the weight of the word 'There', emphatically placed as the trochaic opening of the line, makes clear that it refers back to 'above' and is the antithesis of 'this world'). What can he do? Try the effect of repentance? But he cannot repent. Shakespeare here represents the process of prayer, or rather he dramatises the dilemma which Claudius seeks to resolve by prayer. A part at least of that dilemma is known to every one of us in the audience who is honest with himself—**May one be pardon'd, and retain th'offence?** And the process of Claudius's prayer continues all through Hamlet's subsequent soliloquy. We do not know the result of the King's prayers—**All may be well,** for all we know—until after Hamlet has left the Stage: and when Hamlet speaks of his Uncle as engaged in 'the purging of his Soul', we feel at that moment that the struggle is still on: Lowin, the actor who plays Claudius, by the force of his speech and by his posture afterwards, contributes to this effect. Meanwhile we may once again admire the rightness of Shakespeare's expression: the deliberate pace and the steady but strenuous pulse of the rhythm sustain the illusion of conscience wrestling towards prayer; Claudius's inward conflict is expressed in the structure of the speech, which is that of theological dialectic. At first as the self-searching questions multiply, there seems to be hope: **Then I'll look up, My fault is past.** But when the answers come, they are uncompromising, and the pace of the repeated questions quickens and the last frantic exchange leads to the climax of rhetorical apostrophe:

What then? What rests?
Try what Repentance can. What can it not?
Yet what can it, when one can not repent?
Oh wretched state! Oh bosom, black as death![22]

[73-98] The King bows his stubborn knees at the prie-dieu in the Study, and the story continues upon its expected course, for Hamlet comes racing round the perimeter, making for the Door which will lead him on his upward errand to his mother's closet, the Door by which Polonius has just left the presence of the King. In the following scene, according to the Folio text, just before he bursts into the Queen's presence, he is muttering urgently, *within*, 'Mother, mother, mother': it is possible that at this moment too the word is on Burbage's lips, identifying the swift direction of his journey. But suddenly, as he reaches the farther Post, his urgent haste is halted: for he has caught sight of his enemy, here and now at his mercy and unaware of his danger.

Now might I do it pat. . . . We realise perhaps for the first time that this is the expected revenge: no police-arrest and judicial arraignment, but stark assassination is the way to execute the Ghost's command. **And now I'll do't**—the sword is half-way out of the scabbard. But then the native hue of resolution is sicklied o'er with the pale cast of thought, and he hesitates: **that would be scann'd.** The pause after the words **I, his sole Son, do this same Villain send To heaven** (clearly indicated in the lineation of Q2, which leaves the rest of the pentameter after 'To heaven' empty) marks the struggle of indecision in Hamlet's mind. Close to the front rails of the Stage, he debates with us in the audience the ironical contrast of his father's death, sent to his account with all his imperfections on his head, and his Uncle's case, taken **in the purging of his Soul, When he is fit and season'd for his passage.** And the sword goes back into its sheath, and the avenger consoles himself with eloquent invective—no less violent for the need to whisper it—against the vices of his intended victim. It is no good our throwing up our hands and uncritically calculating how many lives would have been spared if Hamlet had killed his Uncle at this moment. Doctor Johnson's famous observation on this passage should be recorded here: 'This speech, in which Hamlet, represented as a virtuous character, is not content with taking blood for blood, but contrives damnation for the man that he would punish, is too horrible to be read or uttered.' But it is not Shakespeare's habit to make such judgements: and when we consider the effect of the scene upon the sensibilities of the audience, we must remember that, while Claudius kneels in prayer, Hamlet's rage is an extension of the hysteria of I.v, reminding us of the pathos and horror of the Ghost's description of his brother's ultimate villainy.* As to the suggestion of missed opportunity, that is not how the moment appears in Burbage's performance. Since Hamlet pauses to reflect—and as Shakespeare presents him to us, his nature is to reflect—he cannot come to any other conclusion: he cannot kill his enemy at his prayers. Hamlet being what he is, there is no opportunity here, and the story must go on to the wholesale tragedy of its end. It is only after he has gone swiftly off to find his mother, that the full irony of the situation is made clear by the King's brief couplet which shows that his guilt is still stronger than his intention to repent. The Study-curtains close on the unredeemed sinner's frustration:

My words fly up, my thoughts remain below,
Words without thoughts, never to Heaven go.

*   *   *

[III.iv]   And at once the curtains of the Chamber are thrown open. The few furnishings (including the arras behind which Polonius will hide as prearranged) suggest the Queen's closet. Polonius and Hamlet enter, as visitors, from one side: the Ghost, and later Claudius, use the opposite entry, as privileged to walk in the privacy of this apartment.

[1-33]   We have been excitedly awaiting this confrontation of mother and son, but we are hardly prepared for the dramatic violence of the next few moments. Polonius enters in haste—the Prince is on his way—but is not too hurried to give the Queen his last-minute advice, determined that his stratagem should not fail through her maternal indulgence: **Look you lay home to him.** And even as he

* See *pages 50-1, above.*

93

moves towards his hiding-place (**I'll silence me e'en here**), he cannot resist the temptation to reiterate his injunction: **Pray you be round with him**. We hear Hamlet's **Mother, mother, mother**, and the old man darts behind the arras. The interview begins in heat, Gertrude trying her utmost to be round with him, and Hamlet translating in bitter parody each phrase of his mother's rebuke:

—Hamlet, thou has thy Father much offended.
—Mother, you have my Father much offended.

Stung by the insults of his counter-attack, she rises as if to go and fetch Claudius, but he seizes her wrist and thrusts her roughly down upon a chair (**sit you down, you shall not budge**), determined to speak daggers to her, while using none. But the violence of this mad-man, who has through the Players obliquely threatened the King with murder, frightens her: **thou wilt not murther me?** She calls for help, and Polonius behind the arras echoes her cry. In an instant Hamlet whips out his sword and plunges it through the curtain. So much for indecision! And his intention is plain: **is it the King?** (for here he would be 'about some act   That has no relish of salvation in't'). We notice too Gertrude's astonishment in her cry **As kill a King?** which exonerates her, for good and all, from complicity in her late husband's murder. Then he draws aside the curtain and sees what he has done. His contemptuous dismissal of the **intruding fool** is coloured by his chagrin because he has not killed his **Better**.

[34-102]   And thinking no more, as yet, of the consequences of his deed, he turns to his mother who is wringing her hands, and sets about the business of wringing her heart. **What have I done . . . ?** she says, and he roars aloud the enormity of her **Act** which has degraded the sacred vow of marriage; **what act . . . ?** she cries again, as if all she had done was to become her 'Husband's Brother's wife' rather soon after his unfortunate death. What act? The simple answer is adultery: for if the Ghost's word is to be trusted, Hamlet now knows that she was seduced by Claudius before her husband died. But bent on wring-ing her heart (as indeed Shakespeare is bent on wringing ours) Hamlet presents her crime in the vivid pictorial terms of poetic drama. There

is no question here of a family portrait-gallery in the Queen's closet, nor of miniatures pendent round the necks of son and wife. Rather, this is a regular feature of the technique of Shakespeare's poetic drama, to present a picture so vividly to the mind's eye of the audience that it becomes part of the substance of the play.* We remember that Gertrude (the boy Crosse) is sitting. Burbage, over her shoulder, paints in the air (looking straight out into the playhouse) a portrait of Hamlet's father; then, over the other shoulder, a contrasting picture of Claudius. Few things in the play are more beautiful than Hamlet's presentation of his father: for the time being the actor forgets the Queen's presence, and shows by mime and gesture (rather as a producer will show an actor what the author means) what King Hamlet was like: Shakespeare's evocation is not precisely visual, but each physical detail—the hair, the forehead, the eye, the stance—is invested with the grace and grandeur of the synod of gods, who together **give the world assurance of a man.** And we hear the echoes of Hamlet's earlier tributes to his father, 'Hyperion to a Satyr' and 'He was a man, take him for all in all: I shall not look upon his like again' (I.ii.140, 187 f.). All Hamlet's love and admiration for his father are expressed in this passage, and his sorrow for his death. Then, with the transition most skilfully made by the contrast of **This was your Husband** with **Here is your Husband** (the two phrases deliberately placed in parallel position in the verse), he passes to his incredulous disgust at his mother's preference. The torrent of his eloquence is channelled (as in some previous passages†) through the urgent repetition of similar phrases: **Have you eyes? . . . Ha? Have you eyes? . . . sense sure you have . . . but sure that sense Is apoplext . . . Eyes without feeling . . . Ears without hands, or eyes . . . Or but a sickly part of one true sense Could not so mope.** The fuller version of Q2 by no means checks the impulsive flow of Hamlet's tirade, and it continues uninhibited by the counterpoint of her helpless surrender and pathetic pleading (**O Hamlet, speak no more . . . Oh speak to me no more . . . No more**), through his hideous presentation of her incestuous union and his contemptuous abuse of the **Cutpurse** who stole **the precious**

---

* See *page 57, above,* and *page 119, below.*
† See *pages 37, 51* and *77, above.*

Diadem of Denmark, and on to the astonishing climax of the Ghost's reappearance.

[103-135] Astonished we are. No one (unless he has seen the play before) can be expecting this entry. And yet how natural it is that he should be here in this room: and the capricious First Quarto text earns our gratitude by telling us: *Enter the ghost in his night gowne*: no full armour, as on the battlements, but, as Hamlet later tells us, **in his habit, as he lived**. It is a domestic scene, conjuring up briefly for the audience a suggestion of family life which the narrative of the play does not admit, but which is always implicit in Hamlet's grief at his father's death and his mother's 'o'er-hasty Marriage'. And as father, mother and son appear together for the only time in the play, the **gracious figure** of old Hamlet is invested for us with the details of his son's recent loving description ('See what a grace was seated on this Brow . . .'). But alas! one of the three is now dead. And in the presence of the Ghost, Hamlet still asks for heavenly protection. And the Queen, seeing no ghost, thinks that her son is mad again. And the Ghost is but a shadow of the noble original of Hamlet's portrait. He has come, as Hamlet guesses, to whet his **almost blunted purpose**: he cannot rest, we must suppose, until he is avenged: **Do not forget** is a pathetic echo of 'remember me'.

But Shakespeare can make still more dramatic material out of the confrontation of wife and dead husband, and we can follow the drama in the very exact phrases with which the poet not only describes (as he must in the conditions of his day-lit playhouse) but also interprets the demeanour of the three participants: the Ghost describes the Queen's amazement and speaks, with sympathy, of her **fighting Soul** —we remember his command to Hamlet that he should contrive naught against his mother; Gertrude's graphic picture of her son tells us of his **staring eyes** and his hair standing on end; and Hamlet's account of the pale glaring and the **piteous action** of his father prepares us for the unique pathos of his departure; clearly Gertrude's uncompromising protest that she can **see nothing there** and hear **nothing but ourselves** is the immediate reason why the Ghost **steals away**. In many phrases of earlier scenes in the play Shakespeare has built up the character of old King Hamlet, both alive and dead, in our affections, and we feel poignant regret at his parting discomfiture: the poet himself, if tradition is true, joined Burbage and the boy Crosse in the handling of this scene.

[**136-172**] Gertrude, who has been quite unaware of the Ghost's presence, thinks that it is Hamlet's madness (**ecstasy**) which has made him see what is not there. His denial is indignant, and he will not allow her this way of escape:

> **Lay not that flattering Unction to your soul,**
> **That not your trespass, but my madness speaks.**

The Ghost has commanded him to 'step between her, and her fighting Soul': so now he must try to rescue her from her sin: to do this he must persuade her that he is not mad. She must confess to heaven and repent and reform; his metaphors of **Ulcerous** sores and weeds which corruption makes **rank** are part of the pervasive imagery of the play.[23] He is urgent with her not to go to his Uncle's bed: he argues that the habit of abstinence will make it progressively easier to refrain. The repetition of **Good night . . . once more goodnight . . . so again, good night . . .** and again at the end of the scene, **Good night Mother,** hints to us of earlier days when the son would say goodnight to his mother before going off to sleep; and this mood (since the framework of the scene is throughout intimate and domestic) is reflected in the unexpected sequel to **And when you are desirous to be blest**—the sudden charm of **I'll blessing beg of you.**

[**172-199**] Hamlet's moods shift with the bewildering variations of a kaleidoscope. A glance at Polonius behind the arras brings back the reality of the old man's death. His rage gone, Hamlet speaks with dignity and penitence, rather than with a strong sense of personal compassion:

> **For this same Lord,**
> **I do repent: but heaven hath pleas'd it so,**
> **To punish me with this, and this with me,**
> **That I must be their Scourge and Minister.**
> **I will bestow him, and will answer well**
> **The death I gave him.**

He expresses his consciousness of the role he must play in these corrupt times with more resignation than in his earlier cry of 'Oh cursed spite, That ever I was born to set it right' (I.v.188 f.). But there is too a growing realisation of the political difficulties which the death of Polonius will cause: and this reminds him of the danger of his position in his duel with the King. So there is an abrupt reversal of his momentary tenderness towards his mother, and he is once again savagely voicing his disgust, as he imagines how Claudius in amorous vein could wheedle out of her the fact that her son's madness is only a diplomatic pretence. Do tell him, he says, for this is just the sort of important secret that a Queen should betray to **a Paddock . . . a Bat, a Gib**. Whipped by his sarcasm, she promises she will not tell Claudius: and we shall watch in the sequel to see if the lady keeps her word.

[200-217] We hear again of the plan to send Hamlet **to England**. He himself knows of it, and (in the fuller version of Q2) has secret information of the King's sinister intentions; and that Rosencrantz and Guildenstern are to carry **letters seal'd**. He has his own plans of counter-attack (to **delve one yard below their mines, And blow them at the Moon**); and Hamlet, so often considered indecisive, shows a positive relish in the game of active stratagem: **the sport** finds its consummation in the swift and decisive action on board ship, which he recounts in V.ii.12 ff. Now that the success of his plot to catch the conscience of the King has set events moving again, he finds that

> **'tis most sweet**
> **When in one line two crafts directly meet.**

He turns again to Polonius's body and with scant ceremony proceeds to drag it away: for one moment, we think he will give him a generous epitaph, as he describes the still, secret gravity of death: is our last vision of Polonius to be a dignified one? But then he cannot resist the temptation to a contemptuous jingle:

> **Indeed this Counsellor**
> **Is now most still, most secret, and most grave,**
> **Who was in life, a foolish prating Knave.**

And with a last repetition of **Good night Mother,** he is gone, lugging the guts into the neighbour room.

*   *   *

[IV.i] At this point Q2 has: *Eenter King, and Queene, with Rosencraus and Guyldensterne;* the strong implication is that a new scene begins. The Queen dismisses Rosencrantz and Guildenstern (at *line 4*) with **Bestow this place on us a little while.** Many modern editors recognise the suggestion with a new scene and a fresh locality. However the Folio reads simply: *Exit Hamlet tugging in Polonius. Enter King;* the Queen's line of dismissal is omitted, and Rosencrantz and Guildenstern do not appear until *line 32.* This suggests that the King's interrogation of Gertrude follows upon the closet-scene without a break. It is interesting that the First Quarto, which, however untrustworthy textually, may represent a visual memory, reads: *Exit Hamlet with the dead body. Enter the King and Lordes.* And the King is made to say 'Now Gertred, what sayes our sonne, how doe you finde him?' The Folio version, presumably reflecting a later practice, seems the more logical, in its implication that the scene of Gertrude in her closet simply continues after the departure of Hamlet. The pace of the action at this point in the play is rapid, and there is no break in the continuity.

[1-45] Left alone for a moment before the King's appearance, the Queen is distraught with anxiety: she is not weeping, but heaving her breath in deep **sighs**: the King's description of her state aptly portrays the agitation of one who is at a loss what to do. The dilemma is urgent: shall she keep her promise to Hamlet, or shall she tell her husband the truth? She makes up her mind quickly:

—**What Gertrude? How does Hamlet?**
—**Mad as the Seas, and wind . . .**

We are glad to hear her speak a kind word about the **good old man,** but to Claudius Polonius's death is chiefly a warning of his own danger; we shall be blamed, he thinks, and the madman is still at large: **Where is he gone?** Gertrude, we notice, even goes out of her way to embroider Hamlet's madness by inventing a few tears of repentance: **He weeps for what is done.** With his usual prompt resolution the King summons Rosencrantz and Guildenstern and sends them to find Hamlet: they are to **speak fair**, humouring the madman; and to **bring the body Into the Chapel.** Meanwhile the King's **wisest friends**, some of whom we saw at the council-table in I.ii receiving thanks for their acquiescence, are to be called up to discuss this new emergency, which fills the King's soul with **discord and dismay,** less for the madness of his nephew or the death of his minister than for the danger that his good name might be wounded by the news of the deed.

* * *

[IV.ii.1-33] The Chamber-curtains are closed, and the thrilling game of hide-and-seek continues on the lower level, Hamlet darting in (according to the pattern of locality) by the Door through which he had ascended to his mother's closet. He dusts his hands with macabre relish, having **safely stowed** the body of Polonius, and hearing his pursuers, takes up a posture of anticipation: **Oh here they come.** Rosencrantz and Guildenstern follow close at his heels and fence him in on either side. Rosencrantz, who once before (III.ii.345) seemed to be the more positive of the two, leads the interrogation; but Hamlet is in his element, mercilessly parrying and counter-thrusting from the cover of his antic disposition; from callous jesting about the body of his victim he turns to a cruel attack upon his questioner, the sycophant, the **Sponge,** whom his employer will cast aside when he has served his purpose: **when he needs what you have glean'd, it is but squeezing you, and Sponge you shall be dry again.** In the end, when Rosencrantz motions him to **go with us to the King,** he seems for a moment to acquiesce—and then, in a puckish prank, darts out instead by the opposite Door. They two follow him, hunting the hiding fox.

* * *

[IV.iii.1-60] The Study-curtains are thrown open and without pause, the King hurries in, accompanied by some of the less agile of his 'wisest friends' at the rear of the chase. The curtains have revealed the council-table of I.ii; for the tone of interrogation in the King's first question to Hamlet (**Now Hamlet, where's Polonius?**) suggests a formal arraignment. While waiting for his nephew's arrival, the King outlines the political issue, and we learn that, though the court is solidly behind him, he cannot give summary punishment to the Prince, because of his popularity with the **multitude**: the plan to send him abroad remains the wisest policy; indeed that the King is aware of an approaching crisis is apparent in his admission that the problem will be solved by this **desperate** measure **Or not at all**. Rosencrantz reports that, though Hamlet will not tell them where Polonius's body is, he himself is under guard, awaiting the King's pleasure. He is led in, and the King takes his seat as inquisitor at the table. In answer to the King's questioning, his witty insults—the last and most extravagant example of his antic disposition—show scant respect for either his dead victim or his living enemy. With gruesome wit he speaks of Polonius **At Supper . . . Not where he eats, but where he is eaten**, and develops the idea into an oblique impertinence to Claudius, showing how **Your fat King** may by way of worm **go a Progress through the guts of a Beggar** (he himself is the **lean Beggar** who lacks advancement: and we remember his sardonic apology to his school-friends, 'Beggar that I am . . .'). **Alas, alas**, spoken *aside* to one of the councillors, suggests that the King still thinks his nephew mad, or rather that he would like his supporters to think so. He will not allow Hamlet's fencing to move him to anger: there is a sharpness in the reiteration of his first question, **Where is Polonius?** But Hamlet's reply, directly insolent and implicitly menacing, receives no rebuke: **In heaven, send thither to see. If your Messenger find him not there, seek him i'th'other place yourself.** Suddenly, with another macabre pleasantry, Hamlet capitulates and reveals the whereabouts of the body. A hint that the scene of the Queen's closet and Polonius's death was played above in the Chamber, appears in his words, **you shall nose him as you go up the stairs into the Lobby.** The first battle of the interview over, the King pronounces sentence: silkily he explains that his concern is for his nephew's **especial safety.** His balanced phrases grow rapidly towards the climax of the surprise he has prepared for the recalcitrant Prince:

The Bark is ready, and the wind at help,
Th'Associates tend, and every thing is bent
For England.

It is no surprise, as we know. In a quick-fire exchange Hamlet sar-
donically feigns astonishment and Claudius offers veiled warning:

—For England?
—Ay Hamlet.
—Good.
—So is it, if thou knew'st our purposes.

There is a kind of hidden understanding between these adversaries,
which excludes the uncomprehending courtiers. If the council-table
reminds us of I.ii and the first duel between Hamlet and Claudius, it
will strengthen the echo of that earlier scene in the exchange of trenchant mockery and false affection between the two:

—Farewell dear Mother.
—Thy loving Father, Hamlet.
—My Mother: Father and Mother is man and wife: man
and wife is one flesh, and so my mother.[24]

The duel has reached a new stage; the iteration **For England . . . but
come, for England . . . Come, for England** prepares us to anticipate
the sequel. Rosencrantz and Guildenstern are sent after Hamlet, with
instructions that they must sail with him **tonight**: and the King is left
alone, still sitting at the table.

[**61-71**] Through the device of soliloquy, his purpose is made
entirely clear to us for the first time. He tells us that England, smarting
under the wounds of a Danish invasion, owes **homage** to Denmark,
and can hardly disregard the instructions conveyed in a sealed letter
by Rosencrantz and Guildenstern for **the present death of Hamlet.**
He will not be content until he hears that his order has been carried
out; and the imagery of hidden disease expresses the intensity of his
feelings:

Do it England,
For like the Hectic in my blood he rages . . .

The Study-curtains close on this new instance of Claudius's state-craft,
or villainy.

*   *   *

[IV.iv] The next scene in the Folio runs to no more than ten lines:
the bulk of the scene—and it may be thought, its main dramatic purpose—appears only in Q2. What are we to make of this? It looks as
if, by the time Heminges and Condell were assembling their copy in
1623, it was common stage-practice to omit Hamlet's talk with the
Captain and his subsequent soliloquy: it is as if the players thought that
Hamlet had talked enough in private conversation with the audience.
Both Q2 and the Folio agree that Fortinbras must be seen at this point:
it is a long time since we heard anything about him: we were told,
in II.ii.61 ff., that his planned attack upon Denmark, to recover his
father's lost territories, had been diverted to Poland: his levies, his
'list of lawless resolutes' (I.i.98), must be given occupation; they, and
their leader, are ambitious, and honour must be satisfied. It is important
that we should now be reminded of this element in the story, lest his
return from Poland at the end of the play should lack plausibility: it
is important for the same reason that we should *see* Fortinbras now.
But Shakespeare, as so often, turns necessity into opportunity, and
makes dramatic capital out of narrative exposition.

[1-31] Let us see what was the effect of playing the whole scene
as in Q2. As soon as the Study-curtains have closed on the King, *Enter*
Fortinbrasse with his Army over the stage. A marching drum strikes up
(the hint is in the First Quarto's direction, *Enter Fortenbrasse, Drumme*
and Souldiers: we shall recognise the rhythm again at the end of the
play); then marching soldiers (a token army—the Chorus in HENRY V,
from whose speeches much can be deduced about stage-practice,
modestly tells us of 'four or five most vile and ragged foils' who
represented a whole army) follow their Captain into the Doorway;
all, being Norwegian, are wearing a uniform that is strange to us,
different from that of the Switzers who attend the Danish King;

banners add to the military splendour of the scene. Almost simultaneously, but a little later, from the opposite Door come two or three sailors, in sea-caps and sea-boots, carrying an oar, a chest, a coil of rope; at sight of the army, they stop at the back of the Stage, grounding their chest and, during Fortinbras's words, looking back for the arrival of the rest of their company; it is clear that this is a chance meeting of two travelling parties, and that the bare Stage now represents open country.

Fortinbras, every inch a Prince, sends the Captain with a message for the Danish King, at the same time announcing himself for our benefit and reminding us of his purpose; meanwhile, towards the end of the colloquy, Hamlet has followed the sailors on to the Stage, his sea-gown scarf'd about him, and becomes aware of the army marching away. Rosencrantz and Guildenstern, also dressed for travel, are at his heels. The exact meaning of the occasionally recurrent direction, *over the Stage*, is disputed; but it seems natural to interpret Q2 here as indicating that Fortinbras departs through the Door opposite to the one by which he entered; he and his soldiers ignore the unknown travellers, but the spectacle of their passage makes a deep impression upon the watching Hamlet, and he forestalls the departure of the Captain. This officer has some of that individuality which Shakespeare liked to bestow upon his minor characters, and his sceptical account of his general's enterprise sparks off Hamlet's incredulous astonishment:

> **—Truly to speak, and with no addition,**
> **We go to gain a little patch of ground**
> **That hath in it no profit but the name.**
> **To pay five ducats, five, I would not farm it . . .**
> **—Why then the Polack never will defend it.**

The Captain, civilly thanked and quite unaware of the identity of his questioner, goes out by the Door through which Hamlet and his party entered—he is on his way to the Danish court. Rosencrantz and Guildenstern signal to the sailors to pick up their load and, when Hamlet proposes to linger, reluctantly follow them towards the sea-shore.

[32-66] Hamlet, we must remember, has been seemingly out-manoeuvred by the King, and if he were to depart thus tamely with his escort, sailing away from Denmark and the possibility of revenge, he would seem to his audience (so perhaps Shakespeare reflected) to be acquiescing in defeat and allowing fate to take its course. What then is needed at this point? In the first place, the Hamlet we have most lately seen has been callously lugging the guts of Polonius, cruelly taunting Rosencrantz, exercising his wits with the tasteless humour of politic worms and maggots, and baiting Claudius with the iterated ambiguity of father-mother. We are now to witness the bitter aftermath of his antic disposition; he is absent from the Stage, while the pathos of Ophelia's madness and the loyal rage of Laertes play dangerously with our sympathies. It is important, therefore, that before he withdraws from our immediate attention, there should be some restoration of the nobility of one who was once 'th'observ'd of all Observers' (III.i.163). This soliloquy is entirely sane and controlled in its self-analysis, and in its speculation about the nature of man with his **god-like reason** and about the right property of greatness. More important still, we need an assurance that he is resolute, that he will not let things drift: and this is just what the soliloquy gives us. There is, truly, a trace of repetition here: we have heard on a previous occasion of 'a beast that wants discourse of Reason' (I.ii.150); **Even for an Egg-shell** seems to echo 'And all for nothing? For Hecuba!' (II.ii.591 f.). The situation too is familiar. As before a Player's set-piece or a book of philosophy, so now a chance encounter with a soldier turns the thoughts of this hyper-sensitive Prince to his own position, and in his self-questioning he again construes his enforced inaction as his own failure: **Bestial oblivion**, or the **craven** expedient of **thinking too precisely on th'event**; again he calls himself **coward**; again he exhorts himself to action, since he has **cause, and will, and strength, and means To do't**. But there is a difference: the Player who wept for Hecuba was an actor, pretending what he did not feel: Fortinbras is a real person, indeed an important figure in the political life of Hamlet's times, a **delicate and tender Prince** like himself, whose spirit is **with divine ambition puff'd**. Honour is the quest of Fortinbras and his army, and though the objective is an abstract fantasy, they go for it without hesitation, while Hamlet, with every motive for determined action, lets **all sleep**. The fundamental dilemma of whether it is nobler to endure or to act is once more raised,* and on this occasion there is only one conclusion to this reasoning:

> **from this time forth,**
> **My thoughts be bloody, or be nothing worth.**

And he strides resolutely out, on his way to the sea-shore and the boat which will carry him to England. In this way the narrative remains buoyant. In the best tradition of the revenge-tale, the author has placed an apparently impassable obstacle in the way of the accomplishment of his hero's fell purpose; and so the audience is left with a dilemma: the sequence of events since the Mouse-trap play has steadily intensified our sense of Hamlet's growing resolution, and the crown of this sequence is the meeting with Fortinbras and the soliloquy with its ringing decision; but is this empty braggadocio? What can he do on the high seas to defeat his Uncle's purpose? Thus we have a rising sense of expectation, and we are not left to feel that the story of Hamlet has been clumsily allowed to peter out in order to give place for a time to the story of Ophelia. Though the Prince will be absent from the Stage for more than a dozen Quarto pages, it will not be long before we hear news of the issue of his bloody thoughts.[25]

*   *   *

[IV.v.1-20]   The Study-curtains are opened again, and the hangings disclosed remind us of 'the Lobby' which was the background of the long sequence of II.ii. Both Q2 and the Folio insist on Horatio's presence in the following scene, and if we seek for motivation, perhaps we are meant to think that he is watching Hamlet's interests in his absence. By the date of the Folio, it was evidently the practice for Horatio to speak the lines which are ascribed by Q2 to an anonymous Gentleman, perhaps because the actor's skill in speaking was needed for the introductory description of the first thirteen lines. In Q2, after the Gentleman's account of Ophelia, it is Horatio who speaks the three lines beginning **'Twere good she were spoken with . . .**: in the

---

* See *pages 74-5, above.*

Folio, where the descriptive speech is ascribed to Horatio, it is the Queen who has these three lines.*

Shakespeare wants to guide our understanding of Ophelia's words before she appears, to move us, like her other hearers, **to Collection,** to guess at her meaning. The entry of the Queen and her companions is from the Study, marking the change of locality, differentiating the interior of the palace from the open-air setting of the previous scene (placed on the main Stage, with the Doors representing the direction to and from the court of Denmark): once the dialogue begins, the actors move forward and the whole Stage takes on the locality suggested by the hangings in the Study. The Queen, we notice, is as agitated as when we last saw her; she would like to turn her back on unpleasantness and, when persuaded that **'twere good she were spoken with,** forebodes disaster in her guilty soul; the self-condemnation of this revealing *aside* is the result of the progress of events since her uncomprehending question at the beginning of the closet-scene, 'What have I done . . . ?'.

[21-74] Once again, the graphic stage-direction of the First Quarto is valuable: *Enter Ofelia playing on a Lute, and her haire downe singing.* Staring without recognition at the Queen, she asks **Where is the beauteous Majesty of Denmark?** and begins to sing her snatches of ballad-verse. Their basis is no doubt traditional, but she distorts the words to express the thoughts that are uppermost in her mind ('Though nothing sure, yet much unhappily'). She does not like to be interrupted and turns quite sharply on the Queen, bidding her **pray you mark.** With poignant inconsequence she harps upon the two blows which have destroyed her sanity, unpredictably turning from one to the other: as we have been warned, she 'speaks much of her Father' (we learn later of his 'obscure burial'; it seems now that her thoughts are running upon this theme, as she sings of unwept death); and she seems to remember too Hamlet whom she loved, whose letters she returned, who was incomprehensibly cruel to her. Claudius enters from the Study, and Gertrude runs to him with a warning whisper, **Alas, look here my Lord.** He tries to address Ophelia, and it is noticeable that she responds to him with a kind of coy grace;

* See *page 30, above.*

her comment upon the story of the baker's dishonest daughter hauntingly expresses the irony at the heart of tragedy; it is her own case and her father's: **Lord, we know what we are, but know not what we may be.** But when Claudius interprets her words as **conceit upon her Father,** she is sharp again; he is not to speak on that topic: and she changes the subject in her second song, the ballad of **Saint Valentine's day,** which she sings to a vigorous tune,[26] making the points of the story by dramatic changes of pitch and tempo, once again impatient of interruption, and concluding with a lively rendering of a betrayed girl's reproach and her young man's callous response:

> **Quoth she, before you tumbled me,**
> **You promis'd me to Wed:**
> **So would I ha' done by yonder Sun,**
> **An thou hadst not come to my bed.**

There is no reason to infer from this ballad of desertion that in the implied past history of the play Hamlet has seduced Ophelia: such a supposition would be entirely out of key with the character of Hamlet as Shakespeare presents him to us. The natural interpretation of Shakespeare's intention is that, driven out of her mind by Hamlet's treatment of her and the appalling fact that he has killed her father, she has allowed her morbid imagination to play round the words that were spoken the last time they were alone together:

> 'I did love you once.'
> 'Indeed my Lord, you made me believe so.'
> 'You should not have believed me. For virtue cannot so inoculate our old stock, but we shall relish of it. I loved you not.'
> 'I was the more deceived.'

There is also a recollection of Hamlet's ribald taunting of her during the Mouse-trap play scene. And next moment her mind goes back to her father. Infinitely pathetic is her resignation (**We must be patient**), followed by her weeping (**to think they should lay him i'th'cold ground**); but then she startles us again with her sudden sharp tone—

My brother shall know of it—and the King and Queen exchange uneasy glances. Back in the Study, with elaborate dignity (fancying herself perhaps the Prince's wife) she mimes her entry into her **Coach,** and bows her **Goodnight** to all the **Ladies** present—though there be but one.

[**75-96**] The King who, in Hamlet's absence, becomes the mainspring of the action, sends Horatio to keep a close watch on Ophelia. Then he turns to the Queen, lamenting in detail the multitude of troubles that have come upon them. His summary is necessary to prepare us for the next phase of the story, but Shakespeare is never content with a bald exposition: we notice that, although Claudius appeals with an almost pathetic urgency for his wife's sympathy (**Oh Gertrude, Gertrude** . . . and again at the climax **O my dear Gertrude** . . .), when he speaks of her son as **the most violent Author Of his own just remove,** he is in fact obliged to conceal from her his own murderous purpose in that remove; we notice that the people are dissatisfied about Polonius's death, and we are surprised to hear that the politic Claudius has been so foolish as to have him buried hastily and secretly, **in hugger mugger** (and Claudius himself is well aware of his folly); last, but by no means least, we are startled by the news that Laertes has returned from Paris, and inevitably we remember what little we know of this young man: his sensible, affectionate advice to Ophelia; the precepts that his father bade him character in his memory (which contained the warning 'Beware Of entrance to a quarrel: but being in Bear't that th' opposed may beware of thee'); the subsequent mission of Reynaldo to reassure his father that the young man was behaving himself properly in Paris. Once again, although the pace of the play is leisurely, a sense of expectancy prevents the narrative from flagging: the lyricism of Ophelia's madness is set against the tone of the approaching climax. Now Laertes has come racing back on hearing of his father's death, and there are plenty of people ready and willing to give him a garbled account of that. The word **Buzzers** is well chosen to help us interpret the gathering murmurs off-stage.

[**96-111**] The *Noise within* is beyond one of the Stage-Doors, and through this the messenger bursts into the royal presence. His speech is typical of the method of the poetic drama: we must not complain that he is too long-winded for the emergency: his function indeed is to create in our mind's eye the emergency of popular revolt. This is the purpose of his comparison of Laertes and his mob breaking through the Switzer guard to the high seas flooding the shore-flats; and to bring their intention more clearly before our imagination, he speaks of the rabble as thinking that **the world were now but to begin**; his dramatisation of their cries, **Laertes shall be King**, is echoed by the mob back-stage, and provides the right background for the entry of Laertes himself.

[III-152] *With others*, says Q2, but by the time of the Folio, it is simply *Enter Laertes*. And the dialogue is designed to save the company the problems of mounting a mob scene (the only one in the play). We hear the breaking down of the doors, this second *Noise within* being interpreted for our benefit by the King himself. The crowd want to follow Laertes into the King's presence, but he persuades them through the Door to **Stand . . . all without**: at most two or three show their faces, and again retire.

The King's presence of mind in dealing with Laertes commands our admiration: so too does Shakespeare's skill in presenting it. The sequence deserves close study: first there is Laertes's outright challenge (**give me my Father**); then the Queen's intervention, and his violent rounding on her; then the King, silent hitherto, asks the young man his imperious question (**What is the cause . . . ?**), telling Gertrude to **Let him go**; there is nothing to fear, he is a king, and this is treason. In Claudius's sangfroid the theme reappears of the sacrosanctity of kingship:* **There's such Divinity doth hedge a King, That Treason can but peep to what it would.** The ethics of tyrannicide were no clearer in Shakespeare's day than they are now; but here the King's moral position is tolerably secure, and he can afford to confront Laertes: he was not directly responsible for the death of Polonius. His reaction to Hamlet's implicit menace was significantly different, the swift expedient of self-preservation. Now as the sequence proceeds, he again asks Laertes **Why . . . ?** and again he tells Gertrude to **Let him go**; then, as Laertes hesitates, he insists:

* See *pages 89-90, above.*

—Speak man.
—Where's my Father?
—Dead.

And though the terrified Gertrude intervenes as if pleading (**But not by him**), Claudius confidently gives Laertes his head:

Let him demand his fill.

Two points are worth noticing, in analysis of the subtle rhythm of this passage: first that it is knit together by the reiteration **Let him go Gertrude ... let him go Gertrude** (in a different position in the line) **... Let him demand his fill**; and secondly that, regardless of Laertes's question and the Queen's hurried interjection, the King's words make a firm pentameter (**Speak man ... Dead ... Let him demand his fill**); this latter may be an accident of rhythm, but it may be Shakespeare's presentation of the King's unflustered control, and the process of his rapid assertion of authority over the enraged youth.

Laertes's tragic position is the mirror of Hamlet's; Hamlet himself is made to speak of the resemblance in V.ii.75 ff.: 'But I am very sorry good Horatio, That to Laertes I forgot my self; For by the image of my Cause, I see The Portraiture of his'. Inevitably we shall be comparing the reactions of the two young men: the impulsiveness of Laertes is a foil to the prolonged self-analysis of Hamlet. The anger of Laertes is an echo of Hamlet's rage when he first heard the revelations of the Ghost, before his enterprise lost the name of action:

> **to this point I stand,**
> **That both the worlds I give to negligence,**
> **Let come what comes: only I'll be reveng'd**
> **Most throughly for my Father.**

The violence of the young man's righteous indignation is gradually reduced by Claudius's humouring sympathy, as, hinting at a distinction between **Friend and Foe**, he offers to explain at leisure how he himself is guiltless of Polonius's death: and we cannot miss the ironical application in his appeasement:

Why now you speak
Like a good Child, and a true Gentleman.

On the lips of the murderer of another good child's father, it is an effrontery: the irony is no less pungent, as he continues:

That I am guiltless of your Father's death . . .

He has gone far towards calming Laertes, when once again we hear a *noise within*. It is a different sound this time: though made by the same mob, it is not clamorous and aggressive, but rather murmuring with embarrassed sympathy at the poor mad girl's condition and indignant at its cause; one voice says audibly **Let her come in**. (The Folio stage-direction reads: *A noise within. Let her come in. Enter Ophelia*. Q2 erroneously ascribes the line 'Let her come in' to Laertes; it seems likely that the compositor misunderstood his copy.)

[153-200] To repeat the shattering effect of the previous mad-scene might seem to be over-taxing the histrionic powers of the boy-actor. But it is the presence of Laertes that makes the repetition possible. And Ophelia herself is not in the same mood as before: her mind is not dwelling on her thwarted love-affair, but seems to be almost wholly concerned with her father's death: indeed she fancies herself to be taking part in his funeral: she moves singing across the Stage in imagined procession (**They bore him bare-fac'd on the Bier**) and stands by the Trap-Door as if by his grave-side (**And on his grave rains many a tear**); she distributes her flowers among the mourners. The effect of this imaginary ceremonial is all the more heart-rending to her brother because she shows no sign of recognising him: she stands in a central position to hand her flowers, and we shall remember this moment later when she herself is being buried in the same Trap-Door which is now at her feet. And in the memory there will be a verbal echo of great poignancy: Laertes once described the transience of Hamlet's love for Ophelia thus: 'A Violet in the youth

of Primy Nature; Forward, not permanent; sweet not lasting' (I.iii. 7 f.); now by the Trap-Door, the imagined grave of her father, in the presence of Laertes, Ophelia echoes this symbol of transience: **I would give you some Violets, but they wither'd all when my Father died**; and later at the grave of his sister, Laertes will repeat the echo in the words: 'Lay her i'th'earth, And from her fair and unpolluted flesh, May Violets spring' (V.i.260 ff.). Indeed the symbolism of Ophelia's flowers has great pathos, **thoughts and remembrance fitted.** Her words **pray love, remember** are a pathetic valediction for her dead father, but to Laertes they are a persuasion to revenge (as indeed was old Hamlet's 'Adieu, Adieu, Remember me'). **Rue** is for Gertrude. It is the **herb of Grace**, an antidote to carnal lust: she must wear her rue **with a difference.** So the hearers on the Stage may 'botch the words up fit to their own thoughts'. We see her now through the eyes of Laertes: it is he that provides the commentary, and it is worth remarking that the words **Thought, and Affliction, Passion, Hell itself: She turns to Favour, and to prettiness** could hardly have been applied to her earlier scene. Our last impression of Ophelia is one of pathetic innocence; just as in a later play, the Doctor's comment on Lady Macbeth's sleep-walking revelations is 'God, God forgive us all', so now Ophelia prays God's mercy not only on her father's soul, but on **all Christian Souls.** And so, with a curtsey to the company, she is gone.

[201-219] Meanwhile the King has been watching her brother's reactions with silent appraisal. He takes the wild outcry of the young man's grief as his cue for making a generous proposal; he will submit to examination by Laertes's **wisest Friends** (we have heard the phrase before, in IV.i.38), and if found guilty, will yield the **Kingdom**, no less, to him by way of **satisfaction**; if not guilty, he will become his partner in finding **due content** for his soul; the murderer will be punished: **where th'offence is, let the great Axe fall**. It seems unlikely that the first half of his proposal will be put seriously to the test. When we next see the King and Laertes, it appears (as far as Shakespeare lets us know) that they have come to an agreement in private.

* * *

[IV.vi.1–35] The Study-curtains close, and the bare Stage suggests no special locality. Horatio enters, followed by an attendant, and we have barely time enough to wonder what part he can play in the story at this point when we hear that there are letters for him brought by **Sea-faring men** (the reading of Q2; the Folio has the less salty 'Saylors'), which must, he guesses, come from Hamlet. Sea-cap and sea-boots turn any actor into a sailor, but Shakespeare gives even this incidental figure a touch of character: **He shall Sir, an't please him** (his reply to Horatio's polite hope that God will bless him) has a nautical bluffness about it, and he wants to be sure that he has found the right man to deliver his letter to. Before opening the letter, Horatio advances to the front of the Stage, to prevent overhearing, and to give us the full benefit of its contents. Hamlet's last soliloquy (omitted in the Folio) has sharpened our curiosity for news of that sea-voyage.

The actor who plays Horatio has already given us proof of his skill in evocation by speech: he becomes now a good raconteur; he makes us listen: and the news is worth the listening. We hear that **these Fellows**, of whom the bluff sailor is a specimen, have letters for the King too. The encounter with the pirate-ship is in the direct line of romantic adventure; and the touch of modest irony in **we put on a compelled Valour** is also in the vein. Moreover the shrewd presence of mind shown in his bargain with the buccaneers fulfils our expectation of an active Hamlet. We have been prepared by the relish of 'I will delve one yard below their mines' and by the resolute 'My thoughts be bloody, or be nothing worth' (III.iv.208; IV.iv.66). We are to expect much more astonishing news, when the two meet: **I have words to speak in thine ear, will make thee dumb**: meanwhile **these good Fellows** will conduct Horatio to a rendezvous (Horatio raises an eyebrow at this point, and looks sideways at the sea-faring man—for he is presumably one of the pirates), for Hamlet, we slowly realise, is back in Denmark and within easy reach of his friend. Finally, there is some mystery concerning Rosencrantz and Guildenstern, who are holding their course for England.

*   *   *

[IV.vii]   During the scene we have just witnessed, the Stage represented no particular locality, and its very bareness made an unobtrusive setting for the brief but vivid picture of the sea-fight; this scene too, where Claudius and Laertes are in close conference, carries no suggestion of locality, and we shall see, when the Queen joins them, how the anonymous structure of the playhouse makes possible a more elaborate evocation of place in the mind's eye. While it is proper for the action of the play to continue unbroken on the main Stage, an alternative suggestion, that the Chamber was used for this scene, has no less dramatic propriety. In this way a telling contrast emerges between the present scene and the more expansive grave-yard scene which follows. Moreover, we learn later (V.i.316) that this episode takes place at night; in the confined space of the Chamber lighted candles increase the sense of intimacy in the dialogue. Whether the Chamberlain's Men used the main Stage or the Chamber, no special stage-dressing is required: the situation, and interaction of personality, become the uncluttered focus of our attention.

[1-35]   In the interval since we last saw them (so the very first lines of the scene make clear), the King has persuaded the young man that his father's killer is his own dangerous enemy too, and he adduces two plausible reasons for his failure to take summary action. The first is his consideration for Hamlet's mother. The terms in which he speaks of Gertrude will be persuasive to Laertes, but they have also their own particular ring of truth:

> **For my self,**
> **My Virtue or my Plague, be it either which,**
> **She's so conjunctive to my life and soul . . .**

There is irony in the King's candid confession. Is his love for Gertrude his virtue or his plague? We remember his struggle for repentance: 'May one be pardon'd, and retain th'offence?' (III.iii.56). The second reason for the King's decision not to attack Hamlet openly is the Prince's popularity with the common people, who **dipping all his Faults in their affection . . . Convert his Gyves to Graces**. It seems that Hamlet, the 'Rose of the fair State', is much loved not only by his friends and fellow-students but by the people too. Laertes's sense of frustration is natural enough, and we feel again that his position is the reflection of Hamlet's: **And so have I a Noble Father lost. . . .** He too is resolute: **. . . my revenge will come.** The King is ready to support Laertes in this resolution and promises action in a phrase which is less vague than it appears: **You shortly shall hear more.** For the King is expecting at any moment to hear of Hamlet's death in England. Though Laertes does not know it yet, the summary action he is demanding will not be necessary. The irony of this first part of the scene is sharply pointed: after the judiciously placed scene of Horatio and the pirate, we in the audience are aware, as the King is not, of the narrative twist which has brought Hamlet back to Denmark.

[36-105] At this very instant, interrupting the King's speech, the news arrives, and it is the more credible because we are already prepared for it. The King is for a moment bewildered, as how should he not be? He is being told no more than that Hamlet has been set **naked** (without baggage) and **alone** (without his escort) on the coast of Denmark, and intends to pay his respects at court tomorrow. This bewilderment is expressed in a volley of uncomprehending questions, and an uncharacteristic plea for advice. But Laertes is delighted by the news, and it is significant that at first he anticipates with pleasure an honest and open confrontation:

> **. . . I shall live and tell him to his teeth;**
> **Thus diddest thou.**

But this enthusiasm is clearly not to Claudius's liking and sets his mind working fast: he prefers some **practice** which may pass for **accident.** His preparation of the ground for his stratagem may seem unnecessarily long, and the editors of the Folio, no doubt again representing later stage-practice, omit some lines (68–81) which appear in Q2: but they are lines which emphasise Hamlet's **envy** of Laertes's reputation as a swordsman, and without them the later reference, that the Norman's report **Did Hamlet so envenom with his Envy** (*line* 103), comes too abruptly to be convincing. We could perhaps have better spared the inflated account of Lamond's equestrian skill, except that it is part of Shakespeare's dramatic realisation of Claudius's expertise in persuasive tempting: we have to be convinced that a man of Laertes's character, however enraged, can be led to consent to a cold-blooded and treacherous murder. And so this digression plausibly develops through hints, hesitations, leading questions, self-justifying aphorisms, to the moment of Laertes's decision. But the passage, as it stands, in full, is dramatically important also to excite our interest in the prospect of a duel between Hamlet and the incensed Laertes: and not only that: it makes Hamlet's agreement to meet Laertes in apparently friendly contest credible. We are meant to believe that Hamlet is really proud of his skill in fencing, and though the description of his being envenomed with envy is over-coloured by his Uncle's malice, he has indeed been made jealous by the talk of Laertes's prowess: he is after all young, and not averse to wearing that **very riband in the cap of youth**. When in a later scene Osric, following the King's instructions, sets 'a double varnish' on the Frenchman's report, Hamlet, in spite of his open contempt for 'this waterfly', is manoeuvred into accepting the King's wager.

[106-162]   **Now out of this**—after his digression, the King comes to calculated hesitation, suspending his sentence in mid-line, and when Laertes asks what he was about to say, starts on a new tack, with his leading questions,

> **Laertes was your Father dear to you?**
> **Or are you like the painting of a sorrow,**
> **A face without a heart?**

and in answer to the indignant counter-question **Why ask you this?** he launches into a wordy philosophical reflection on the mellowing effect of time and the dangers of procrastination: as the actor Lowin delivers this homily, he makes us feel the ironical application to Hamlet's own condition:

> **that we would do,**
> **We should do when we would: for this 'would' changes,**
> **And hath abatements and delays as many**
> **As there are tongues, are hands, are accidents . . .**

Then when audience and victim alike are thoroughly lulled, he pounces (in a repulsive image):

> **but to the quick of th'ulcer:**
> **Hamlet comes back: what would you undertake . . . ?**

Laertes's vindictive answer, with its savage rhythm, is the climax of this long exercise in persuasion:

> **To cut his throat i'th'Church.**

At once Claudius smoothly approves the young man's resolution:

> **No place indeed should murder Sanctuarize;**
> **Revenge should have no bounds.**

It is easy to overlook the exactness of Shakespeare's expression. The familiar phrase in this second line is no cliché but in its context an unscrupulous development of the unexceptionable thought of the preceding line. Moreover it has its ironic application to the main situation of the play: we remember Claudius kneeling in his struggle for repentance and Hamlet's decision to postpone action until a time when there should be no such bounds to his revenge. Claudius's stratagem depends upon his understanding of Hamlet, and we are almost surprised to hear from him at this moment a tribute to his nephew's qualities (at least as they might be in better times), to his **generous** nature, **free from all contriving**. Laertes too is of an open-hearted disposition, but he too is turned against his nature by his grief for a father's death; and so successful is Claudius's method that he not only agrees to the wickedness of using **a Sword unbated** (with no button on the point) but also suggests of his own volition that he should put poison on the sword's point. We have hardly time to consider why, or for that matter how or when, he bought so dangerous a poison, before the King is pondering a means of reinsuring against failure:

> **I'll have prepar'd him**
> **A Chalice for the nonce . . .**

This competition in villainy nearly borders on the melodramatic, but the scene is carried along by the rhythmical variety and urgency of the King's diction.

[163-195]   And if we are tempted to smile, the mood cannot survive the clamorous lamentation which heralds the Queen's unexpected entry. Yet the news of Ophelia's death can hardly surprise us, except in the manner of it; and the manner, when we hear of it, seems perfectly appropriate to the pathos of her condition. This is one of those instances (not rare in Shakespeare) where the speech is more important than the speaker:* its narrative is an essential episode in the plot, a 'necessary Question of the Play', and the details of picture and imagery which create the atmosphere of flowers and music, of the **weeping Brook** and that element to which the drowning girl seemed **like a creature Native, and endued**, must be conveyed with perfect clarity to the mind's eye of the audience. Crosse, the first Gertrude, has been told to concentrate upon this task; it would be villainous and would show a most pitiful ambition, to solicit special attention for the Queen's personal distress. She uses her gesture and miming to help make her tale more graphic, rather than to indicate her own feelings: she is standing close to the rail of the upper level of the Tiring-House, and can look downwards into the **Brook** or up to the **pendent boughs** of the willow that **grows aslant** it; with eye and hand she can sharpen the moment of accident—sudden but not violent, to suit the otherwise gentle tenour of her tale; a simple gesture shows **her clothes spread wide,** and the voice alone, echoing Ophelia's momentary lightness of heart, presents the unforgettable picture of her floating on the surface of the stream and singing her **snatches of old laudes**; for 'laudes' the Folio has the less telling word 'tunes': in the version we owe to Q2 she sings, as she floats contented to her death, hymns of praise: she is indeed **incapable of her own distress.**

The Queen begins her account with the news of Ophelia's death, and Laertes clearly understands, from the beginning, that his sister is **drown'd**. But, in the manner of the poetic drama, the story is evoked for us in its own sequence, and Laertes, following the imaginary picture with his eye, seems to hope up to that last moment when he cries, as

* See *page* 31, *above.*

if understanding for the first time, **Alas then, is she drown'd?** Then, overcome by the story's end, he weeps in spite of himself, and at the same time feels his anger rising in him all over again. The poignant description of his sister's death complements the King's persuasion: the rage which prompts him to murder Hamlet is the more intelligible to us. As Laertes breaks away, to hide his tears, the King expresses to Gertrude the fear that Ophelia's death will frustrate any effort to **calm his rage.** We cannot help noticing the hypocrisy of his words; his wife is not to be told that for Laertes to be incensed is just what he himself wants. The Chamber-curtains close on their departure.

*   *   *

[V.i.1-66] The story continues with the obvious sequel, Ophelia's burial. But Shakespeare's handling of this episode is by no means obvious. We have been long indoors (apart from a brief and almost incidental excursion to the sea-shore), but the atmosphere of the churchyard is economically established. The Study-curtains are opened and disclose properties of a kind akin to those familiar from Henslowe's lists of the stock-in-trade of a rival company, the Admiral's Men—a lych-gate broad enough to accommodate the funeral procession, a yew-tree and a head-stone: some such property-furniture will tell us immediately where we are. But, as we shall see, even without these rudimentary properties, the poet's word places the scene firmly as soon as it begins. Through the lych-gate comes the Sexton's mate, carrying a pick-axe and a spade; after him follows the Sexton himself, pushing his wheelbarrow. As they enter, the Trap-Door in the centre of the Stage is opened from below. The Sexton is Robert Armin: we know him for a clown of character; neither Touchstone nor Feste depended wholly on his verbal wit, but had each his individual personality; now Armin, with Shakespeare's help, is to break new ground, though he retains the disconcerting truthfulness of the 'allow'd fool'. The Sexton's mate is likewise no mere conventional figure of stage-clowning. They establish immediately the relevance of the scene in the play's plot: it is plain that the subject of their discussion is Ophelia, of whose death we have just heard. In the single phrase **make her Grave straight** we are clearly informed of both the function of the clowns and the locality of the scene. In Shakespeare's playhouse the unbroken continuity of performance points this telling juxtaposition of the two scenes.

The matter-of-fact callousness of their argument adds greatly to the verisimilitude of the episode, and makes the right prelude to the tragic issues of its climax. They talk as men will do over their pints at the pub, the Sexton being the acknowledged expert on legal matters, long-winded and contentious, his younger mate surprising us (and him) by the shrewd common-sense of **if this had not been a Gentle-woman, she should have been buried out of Christian Burial**. Conceding the justice of this remark, the Sexton lowers himself into the Trap-Door and calls **Come, my Spade**. Thereafter his actions in digging and shaping and squaring off the grave contribute further to the impression of reality. The riddle too is in character—

> **What is he that builds stronger than either the Mason, the Shipwright, or the Carpenter?**—

with the mate typically quick-witted in his guess of **the Gallows maker**, and then charmingly crestfallen as his inspiration escapes him —**Mass, I cannot tell**; and its dramatic value appears in the Sexton's conclusion, spoken with humorous solemnity, **the Houses that he makes, lasts till Doomsday**. We are not surprised to hear the young man sent off to the local for **a stoup of Liquor**.

[67-125] Meanwhile, quite unexpectedly, Hamlet has appeared in a Doorway; he is wearing his 'sea-gown', and Horatio is with him; so we are quick to understand that the rendezvous suggested in his letter has taken place. The entry by the Door (no door at this moment, but just a means of access to the Stage) makes it clear that they have approached the churchyard from a distance, evidently on their way from the sea-coast to the palace. In Q2 Hamlet and Horatio enter after the first stanza of the Clown's song. The Folio is more helpful in giving the entry on the cue **Mass, I cannot tell**. They overhear the macabre solution to the riddle. The Folio direction reads: *Enter Hamlet and Horatio a farre off*. Busy with his grave-making, the Sexton sings a popular ballad to while away the time, finding some difficulty in

remembering the words. The repetitions at the end of the first line of the first and third stanzas suggest that he cannot remember how the next line begins. The regular metre is discernible in the second stanza. But there are many differences from the original song as it was uncovered by Theobald: the Clown sings his own, not entirely intelligible, version; yet even this is apt enough with its ageless theme of youth and love destroyed by death. Hamlet, in half-amused disgust, comments from the distance (still by the Door): **Has this fellow no feeling for his business, that he sings at Grave-making?** And Horatio's reply clinches the impression we have already formed since the beginning of the scene: **Custom hath made it in him a property of easiness.**

As the Sexton throws up from the newly-dug grave first one skull and then another, and **jowls** them **to th'ground** to emphasise the final rhyme of his stanzas, Hamlet (now on the perimeter of the Stage, in front of a Stage-Post) allows his imagination to play upon the identity of their former owners: one may have been **a Politician** (like Polonius), or **a Courtier** (like Rosencrantz and Guildenstern—**Good Morrow sweet Lord: how dost thou, my good Lord?**). As for these bones—**mine ache to think on't**: it is not the first time that he has contemplated the state of death. All the time Shakespeare's vocabulary is embellishing the graveyard atmosphere—**my Lady Worm's . . . a shrouding-Sheet . . . a Pit of Clay.** Then with characteristic humour, making a counterpoint with the macabre, he (Shakespeare, or Hamlet, or Burbage) aims his irony at that numerous and most intelligent section of his audience: **why might not that be the Skull of a Lawyer?** and his elaborate cadenza on this fancy brings the odour of mortality right into the body of the playhouse.

[125-201] With sudden decision, Hamlet walks up to the end of the open Trap-Door, and accosts the Sexton. His abrupt question **Whose Grave's this Sir?** sets our nerves on edge: for we know the shocking answer. So the Sexton's perverse hedging, the circumlocution of the **absolute** knave, tickles us with the laughter that expresses release from tragic tension. And as Hamlet's curiosity about the dead woman's identity peters out, we are ready for the comedy of the ensuing digression. The whole playhouse laughs spontaneously at the

Sexton's whimsical wit: playwright and players enjoy themselves at the expense of their English audience, and the joke about **young Hamlet** that is **mad, and sent into England**, is as richly apposite in the twentieth century as ever it was: **'Twill not be seen in him there, there the men are as mad as he.** This digression fulfils a purpose in that it places in perspective the great events of the play. We learn that old King Hamlet's defeat of the elder Fortinbras (in a sense, the starting-point of the play's story; and Horatio spoke of it, in I.i, as if of recent history) took place on **the very day, that young Hamlet was born,** and that was **thirty years** ago. During this span of time, the Sexton has worked at his task, **man and Boy,** and politician and courtier alike have found their way to his graves. The implicit calculation of young Hamlet's age is subordinated to the sense of historical perspective and of the littleness of a man's life.

Then Hamlet, with a swift change of mood, and standing now centrally behind the Trap-Door, looking down into it, brings the gruesome horror of burial still more vividly before the mind's eye with his question, **How long will a man lie i'th'earth ere he rot?** We smile still, but somewhat wryly, at the Sexton's practical hints on decomposition; and we are taken unawares by Shakespeare's next dramatic stroke. We have no idea who this **mad Rogue** is whose memory causes the Sexton so much posthumous amusement. But Hamlet's dumbfounded start as he hears the name of his father's **Jester,** brings us up with a jerk: and we watch with a sympathetic fascination the horror on his face as he takes **Yorick's Skull** into his hands.

[201-239] Armin ducks below the level of the Trap-Door, and we forget Horatio's presence, after Burbage has thrown *aside* over his shoulder his incredulous **I knew him Horatio.** In this passage Burbage cannot fail to evoke in our minds the happy days of the Prince's childhood, when he rode pick-a-back on Yorick's shoulders, and kissed his lips, and laughed with a child's delight at his pranks, his songs, his wise-cracks **that were wont to set the Table on a Roar**; and at the same time he makes our gorges rise at the transformation; there are no lips to kiss now; there are no jokes now, though the skull is grinning; there is no jaw, so that, with a tragic quibble, the jester may be said to be **quite chopfall'n.** There is a sudden revulsion of feeling: **Now get you to my Lady's Chamber, and tell her, let her paint an inch thick, to this favour she must come.** In the sardonic line there is the image of frail womanhood ('God hath given you one face, and you make your selves another', III.i.151 f.), of painted Gertrude in her chamber, of the poor girl he once had loved: **Make her laugh at that**—and she, poor Ophelia, 'rest her Soul, she's dead', though he does not know it; and her grave—**my Lady's Chamber,** whither the skull is sent with its gruesome message—is at his feet.

In the end, the whole of this haunting passage is summarised in Hamlet's contemplation of the fate of **Alexander**—Alexander who had been the 'expectancy and Rose' of the ancient world, who died at the height of his glory in his thirty-third year, and who now is merely the 'Quintessence of Dust'. **To what base uses we may return, Horatio.** As the play advances towards its end, words and phrases, sentiments and moods gain added power as they echo the detail of past scenes. In the fancy of Alexander's **dust** and its progress to **a Beer-barrel** there is a reminiscence of the King's progress through the guts of a beggar (IV.iii.33 f.). Hamlet's graveyard thoughts are part of that same *contemptus mundi* (expressed now with a new lightness, even serenity) which has made its intermittent appearance since the beginning of the play—in the first soliloquy, in his melancholy summary of the estate of man (II.ii.323 ff.), in 'To be, or not to be'. It will not be long before Hamlet speaks of the approach of death: 'if it be not now, yet it will come; the readiness is all' (V.ii.235 f.). And at the very last moment he must invite Horatio to forgo the felicity of death and to remain awhile 'in this harsh world' (V.ii.361 f.). This present moment is the richer for its illumination of the relationship of Hamlet and Horatio: the tone is familiar from those occasions when we have heard Hamlet and his fellow-student in conversation: the atmosphere of student talk, the hint of Wittenberg days, is subtly communicated to us: Horatio's part is still to restrain the wilder flights of Hamlet's imagination (earlier examples of Hamlet's extravagant, sometimes morbid, fancy being checked by the laconic Horatio can be found in I.ii.179; I.v.125 f., 133; III.ii.296 ff.):

—'Twere to consider too curiously to consider so.
—No faith, not a jot.

And Hamlet pursues the trail of his fancy to its ultimate absurdity: pleased with his own ingenious logic, he composes an impromptu quatrain to illustrate it, and has just found a rhyme for his cadence, when he is interrupted, perhaps by that uncanny sound, the ringing of a hand-bell in front of a corpse on the way to the churchyard: Ophelia, we discover later, has been allowed 'the bringing home Of Bell and Burial'. Hamlet, like the three 'riotoures' of Chaucer's *Pardoner's Tale*, hears 'a belle clinke Biforn a cors, was caried to his grave'.

[239-244] Meanwhile the grave-digger, who has been putting the final touch to his preparations, wheels his barrow discreetly out of the way. As the cortège moves slowly through the lych-gate, Hamlet (couching with Horatio in the shelter of one of the Doorways) interprets for our benefit the significance of what we are seeing: although the King and Queen are among the mourners, these are **maimed rites**, a scant minimum of ceremonial: this means that the woman was a suicide; clearly she was **of some Estate**, though. The stark bareness of the proceedings—like her father, she is being interred in hugger mugger—makes the occasion seem familiar, and therefore uncanny.

[245-315] Laertes is overwrought: the insistent repetition of his question, **What Ceremony else?**, in face of the Priest's silence shows him to be on the verge of hysteria. The few lines of the Priest's dignified obduracy contain material for a whole chapter from a novel of Elizabethan village life. It is to be noticed that, if the Sexton's mate has got his facts right, the Church takes a different view from the coroner's court: it is also plain that he had good cause for saying that 'if this had not been a Gentlewoman, she should have been buried out of Christian Burial'; the King has intervened to annul the Church's decision. The Priest expresses his disapproval, and the liturgical echoes in his speech add greatly to the solemnity of the atmosphere: the contrast of Laertes's truculent outburst is the more effective: while the bearers lower the coffin into the grave, he turns upon the Priest with scornful abuse:

**A Minist'ring Angel shall my Sister be,
When thou liest howling!**

And this is the moment when Hamlet realises for the first time whose grave this is. The Queen strews flowers into the open grave, and we remember how poor Ophelia herself not long ago was standing at this same spot, distributing (in mad fancy) her flowers at her father's funeral;[27] perhaps the Queen carries rosemary: 'Pray love, remember'; we recall that the violets withered all when her father died, and Laertes has just prayed that **from her fair and unpolluted flesh, May Violets spring.*** The Stage-building and its familiar architectural features quite often prompt this kind of reminiscence by similarities of positioning, posture and gesture. When Gertrude goes on to say **I hop'd thou shouldst have been my Hamlet's wife**, we are surprised (although she has hinted so much once before, at III.i.40) because both Polonius and Laertes have led us to assume that such a marriage was unthinkable. The effect of her words now is doubly dramatic; first upon Hamlet, who has at this very moment heard the news of Ophelia's death, and secondly upon Laertes, to whose enraged spirit Hamlet is the villainous contriver of his whole family's destruction. In his fury, quite unaware, of course, of his adversary's presence, he leaps down into the open grave, and for one horrifying moment we see him catching the dead body of his sister once more in his arms; she has been borne 'bare-fac'd on the Bier'. The gesture is melodramatic—he cannot really intend to be buried alive—and it kindles a sudden explosion of unreasoning anger in Hamlet. With a bravura as extravagant as Laertes's own, he strides into the centre of the group and uncompromisingly declares his return to Denmark: he is **Hamlet the Dane**; it is perhaps a deliberate assumption of the royal nomenclature, as we have heard the phrase used both by Claudius and by Hamlet himself (I.ii.44, I.iv.45). Laertes, astounded by this sudden confrontation, struggles out of the grave and grapples with Hamlet. The Folio tells us in a stage-direction that Laertes *Leaps in the grave*, while Q2 leaves it to be inferred from his words. It is clear from Laertes's violent **The devil take thy soul**, and Hamlet's rejoinder **Thou**

---

* See *page* 113, *above.*

pray'st not well, I pr'ythee take thy fingers from my throat, that it is Laertes who springs first to the attack. There is no justification in either of the good texts for the practice of Hamlet's jumping into the grave: but this inconvenient tradition is supported by the First Quarto's direction *Hamlet leapes in after Leartes*: and the subsequent lines of this perhaps eye-witness text, 'And where thou talk'st of burying thee alive, Here let us stand: and let them throw on us, Whole hills of earth . . .', certainly suggest that both are in the grave. Either method of staging the scene is possible.

Topping the uproar, as the courtiers strive to part the combatants, Hamlet's cry of **I lov'd Ophelia** is a ringing climax. We must take the words as truth, with all their implications in interpreting the previous course of the story. That his scorn and anger betray him into rodomontade, in no way invalidates the sincerity of his outcry: in a later scene (V.ii.79 f.) he explains what happened, in a private conversation with Horatio: 'But sure the bravery of his grief did put me, Into a Tow'ring passion': it is the inflated and melodramatic expression of Laertes's grief, vividly characterised in Hamlet's interpreting verbs, **whine . . . prate . . . mouth,** that provokes from the Prince (who, we know, abhors the 'actions that a man might play', I.ii.84) this outburst of rant. Later he will apologise to Laertes for the failure of his emotional control: and even now he is quick to admit the unseemly futility of his exhibition: **nay, an thou'lt mouth, I'll rant as well as thou.** The interjections of the King and Queen and the other bystanders hardly check the flow of Hamlet's tirade.[28] In the end, with (if we accept the more rational ascription of Q2) the Queen interpreting the swift changes of her son's **Madness** from violence to dejection, Hamlet makes an attempt to reason with Laertes, but meeting with no response, dismisses the histrionic scene with a scornful jingle:

> **Let Hercules himself do what he may,**
> **The Cat will Mew, and Dog will have his day.**

And he stalks away through the lych-gate, followed by Horatio, at the prompting of the King.

[316-321] Claudius has a private word with Laertes, reminding him (and us) of **last night's speech** and preparing us for a quick dénouement. All retire through the lych-gate, the Queen first, to **set some watch** over her son, the King deliberately after his equivocal last lines:

> **This Grave shall have a living Monument:**
> **An hour of quiet shortly shall we see;**
> **Till then, in patience our proceeding be.**

When all have gone, the Sexton wheels his barrow to the grave-side, and with the help of his mate—who returns at this moment with the stoup of liquor from Yaughan—tidies up the grave. The return of normal life rounds off the scene; after they have pushed the barrow-load of tools (and skulls and bones) through the lych-gate, the Study-curtains close, and the shutting of the Trap-Door restores the even surface of the Stage.

*   *   *

[V.ii] The bare Stage, projecting in front of the closed curtains of the Study, is now without locality: and during the powerful narrative of the first part of the next scene it remains so: there is no distraction of time and place while Hamlet evokes for us the dangerous night at sea when, his 'sea-gown scarf'd' about him, he groped 'in the dark' and 'finger'd' the King's commission. But as the crisis of the present time comes close again, the Stage is once more invested (by a few economical touches) with a precise sense of locality. Hamlet's acceptance of the King's wager gives us the first clear sense of place: 'Sir, I will walk here in the Hall'. The anonymous Gentleman who follows Osric echoes the phrase: '. . . you attend him in the hall', and adds that 'the King, and Queen, and all are coming down'. In the First Quarto the Gentleman tells Hamlet that the King and Queen 'Are comming downe into the outward pallace'. So easily does the narrative of Shakespeare's poetic drama slip from the placeless setting which gives opportunity for the free range of the mind's eye to the precise definition necessary for immediate action.

    [1-55] Hamlet and Horatio appear, in the middle of a conversation.

There is a gap in the narrative, which must be filled: we have heard what happened in the engagement with the pirates, but not what went before that: in his letter to Horatio Hamlet hinted that there was 'much to tell' about Rosencrantz and Guildenstern. So the first part of the scene is mere exposition, but vividly and wittily retailed: in this narrative verse there is a rhythmic variety and vigorous diction which suggest Hamlet at his most energetic and decisive. There is no sense of 'the Native hue of Resolution' being 'sicklied o'er, with the pale cast of Thought'; rather **Our indiscretion sometimes serves us well, When our deep plots do pall.** And, as before, Horatio's laconic interjections are endearingly in character.* **Remember it, my Lord?** (could I ever forget the circumstances of your departure to England?)—the fervour of the question quickens our anxious curiosity. Hamlet, like all good story-tellers, knowing the value of calculated digression, enlarges on the recklessness of his adventure and, when he deduces from this that **There's a Divinity that shapes our ends . . . ,** Horatio's solemn nodding assent (**That is most certain**) again hints to us of the student days of philosophic talk. The pace of the narrative can be gauged from the framework of its syntax: **rashly . . . Up from my Cabin . . . Grop'd I . . . had my desire, Finger'd their Packet, and . . . withdrew . . . making so bold . . . to unseal Their grand Commission, where I found . . . an exact command . . . That . . . My head should be struck off.** This outline makes one single sentence, spanning some nineteen lines; and the digressions (reflective, apologetic, explanatory) are swept along by the urgent pace of the narrative. Hamlet gives Horatio **the Commission** to read **at more leisure**, but it seems that Horatio, quite naturally, cannot keep his eyes off this villainous document; for the story-teller twice calls his attention (**wilt thou hear me how I did proceed? . . . wilt thou know Th'effect of what I wrote?**), and in this way the poet artfully ensures our attention too. The topical gibe at the fashionable illegibility of states-men keeps us amused, and so does the parody of diplomatic language (**As . . . As . . . As . . . And many such like Asses of great charge**); and once again vigorous digression leads, through the cumulation of a single sentence, to incisive climax: aided by good fortune and the rapid

* See *page* 124, *above.*

working of his **brains** that need no **Prologue,** Hamlet ensures at one stroke his own safety and the destruction of the spies, the 'Villains' by whom he was 'benetted round'; they, not he, are to be

> **put to sudden death,**
> **Not shriving time allowed.**

We reach the point of the **Sea Fight,** about which we know already, before we have had leisure to grow weary of so volatile and various a reporter.

[56–80] Horatio's pondering **So Guildenstern and Rosencrantz go to't** conveys no explicit judgement, but Hamlet is swift to forestall any critical implication: **They are not near my Conscience.** Rosencrantz and Guildenstern go clumsily, **by their own insinuation,** to their deaths: at this crisis of the story they are simply swept aside; the personal duel between Claudius and Hamlet is swift and ruthless, and it excludes all other considerations: there is no place for morality:

> **'Tis dangerous, when the baser nature comes**
> **Between the pass, and fell incensed points**
> **Of mighty opposites.**

We notice that in the catalogue of the King's villainies Hamlet includes the crime of usurpation; the King has **popp'd in between th'election and my hopes**: and he continues by observing his own personal danger: the enemy has **thrown out his Angle for my proper life.** According to Q2 Osric enters at *line* 67 (**is't not perfect conscience . . . ?**). But the additional thirteen lines in the Folio are valuable in that they dramatically intensify our sense of the decisive Hamlet. Prosser, concerned to show that Hamlet has decided to leave all to the will of Heaven, that in his last moments 'he has fought his way out of hell', argues that this recrudescence of his rage and his callous account of the fate of his schoolfellows are 'among the many contradictions suggesting that Shakespeare did not finish cleaning up the traces of revision'. The argument is unconvincing, however tempting to the moralists. While there is, certainly, a new serenity in the Hamlet of these last scenes, there is nothing to suggest that he has abandoned his decision to kill Claudius. Indeed we find here the final banishing of doubt, the determination **to quit him with this arm**, to destroy **this Canker of our nature**; and when Horatio warns him that the news from England will bring matters to a head, Hamlet reassures him (and us) with his resolute reply:

> **The interim's mine, and a man's life's no more**
> **Than to say 'one'. . .**

The King's life is at the mercy of the single thrust of a rapier.[29] So too in the sequel (by a kind of prospective irony) is Hamlet's. Next moment he touches our hearts again with his sympathetic understanding of Laertes's case:

> **For by the image of my Cause I see**
> **The Portraiture of his . . .**

He too has lost a father. Yet the parallel situations continue to point the differences between the two young men. This very sympathy fills us with misgiving, when we remember what sort of requital Laertes has in store.

[81-202] *Young Osricke*, as he is described in the Folio stage-direction on his first entry (and again by Claudius before the duel), is a 'character-part'—a fop, both in appearance and in speech; in the First Quarto he is called *a Bragart Gentleman*. But he is not altogether a fool. Baldwin allots the part to Cowley who, he suggests, has just played Aguecheek and is about to play Slender. Osric's function in the story makes us take him more seriously than either of these. In an interesting note on V.ii.96–7, Dover Wilson quotes a passage from Webster's Induction to Marston's *The Malcontent*, which is reminiscent of this scene; it is a conversation between members of Shakespeare's company, including Condell and Burbage (who probably played Horatio and Hamlet) and William Sly. It is possible that Sly played Osric, but there is a portrait of him which shows a pronounced personality, and Baldwin argues that he is likely to have played Laertes.

Nevertheless that Shakespeare did not intend Osric to be played as the conventional foolish dandy of farce is made clear by the fact that he allots him a prominent part in the ordering of the duel, and indeed risks allowing him to speak immediately before Hamlet's dying words. At this present moment he has to perform a vitally important task for the King, the sort of job which would earlier have been entrusted to Rosencrantz and Guildenstern. The plan which the King and Laertes have concocted depends entirely upon whether Hamlet can be persuaded to meet Laertes in a fencing-match. Shakespeare's problem is to make Hamlet's agreement seem plausible: at their last meeting the two parted in anger; and anyway any proposal emanating from the King would be treated with suspicion. The former objection is already on the way to being removed; for we have just heard Hamlet express his regret that he forgot himself to Laertes, and his decision to 'court his favours'. The second objection must now be tackled.

Osric, in his comically affected way, carries out the King's instructions faithfully: we know already (from IV.vii.131 ff.) what those instructions are—to praise the excellence of Laertes, and to set a double varnish on the fame the Frenchman Lamond had given him. What better emissary for this purpose than **this waterfly**? Meanwhile Hamlet enjoys himself hugely at his expense, sharing his enjoyment with Horatio (and with us). His caricature of Osric's style, extravagantly embellished in the more expansive version of Q2, is spoken apparently in all seriousness, and bewilders him into unaccustomed silence; even Horatio joins in the baiting of the young man, whose **purse is empty already, all's golden words are spent**. But young Osric does not lose his presence of mind, and sticks doggedly to the trail: he has a mission to fulfil. He proceeds (regardless of Hamlet's teasing interruptions) to praise the **excellence** of Laertes **for his weapon:** his retinue say he has no equal, **he's unfellowed**. This is just the phrase to arouse Hamlet's envy, of which we have already been told by Claudius (IV.vii.102 ff.): a certain hardening in the tone of Burbage's voice marks the instinctive reaction. It does not matter if Osric's eccentric phrasing prevents us from understanding the stakes of the wager: but we must be made to listen—and a sudden change to plain speech helps us to do so—to the terms of the duel: Laertes (who has insisted on 12 bouts instead of the customary 9) must be at least '3 up' at the end to win.[30]

Then, all of a sudden, the crisis of the conversation springs upon us. Hamlet is off his guard, for two reasons—his unthinking contempt for the 'waterfly', and his unconscious jealousy of Laertes's reputation in fencing. **How if I answer no?** is meant to baffle Osric with perverse misunderstanding: but Osric's reply is most shrewdly calculated: **I mean, my Lord, the opposition of your person in trial**. There is a moment of silence—during which we have time to think of the unspoken implication, that honour is involved: surely your lordship would not want me to convey such an answer? Then, with abrupt decision, Hamlet makes his reply: I will be here in the hall: at this time of day I habitually take some exercise: I will do my best to win for the King. He has swallowed the bait, and all his parting mockery (**after what flourish your nature will**) does not conceal from us the fact that Osric is a clever angler, and a successful one.

[203-218]   The entry of an unnamed lord (which appears in Q2 but not in the Folio) is valuable, if not altogether necessary, in bridging the transition between the satirical mockery of Osric and the poignant intimacy of Hamlet's last moments alone with his friend. It also serves to remind us again of the unresolved discord between Hamlet and Laertes: his mother's wish that he should be reconciled before the contest—advice which he unquestioningly approves—sharpens our anxious curiosity about Laertes's likely response.

[219-238]   There is a delicacy of understatement in the sequel which is especially characteristic of the relationship between Hamlet and Horatio. In plain terms, Hamlet has a premonition of death; but Shakespeare is at pains to avoid plain terms. To the prediction that he will **lose this wager**, Hamlet responds with the animation of rivalry. It should be noted that there is no question, at this point, in Hamlet's mind that his match with Laertes is to be a duel to the death. But then immediately his tone changes. Neither he nor Horatio is explicit about the premonition: **how ill all's here about my heart . . . a kind of gain-giving . . . If your mind dislike any thing**—this is as near as they will go. Horatio, even now at the eleventh hour, would postpone the crisis, **forestall** the arrival of the court, make an excuse. But Hamlet

will none of it: **Not a whit, we defy Augury; there's a special Providence in the fall of a sparrow.** Especially moving is the quietness which comes upon Hamlet in the face of the imminent crisis of a reckoning with the King; and it is imminent; as the sense of locality has gathered precision, so too does the sense of a present resolution of the play. The King has sent 'to know if your pleasure hold to play with Laertes, or that you will take longer time'; and Hamlet's reply has serenely accepted that the time has come: 'now or whensoever, provided I be so able as now'. When he goes on to tell us, in his tranquil syllogism, that **if it be now, 'tis not to come**, we understand, without being told, what 'it' is. And he is ready. The brief cadence of Q2 expresses his resignation: **Let be.**

[239-293]   The state entry breaks in on this cadence. The unusually full stage-directions of both Q2 and the Folio make it clear that the last episode of the play begins in pomp. Q2 provides for a fanfare:

> *A table prepard, Trumpets, Drums and officers with Cushions,*
> *King, Queene, and all the state, Foiles, daggers,*
> *and Laertes.*

The Folio adds gauntlets to the foils and gives a precise direction for the table:

> *Enter King, Queene, Laertes and Lords, with other Attendants*
> *with Foyles, and Gauntlets, a Table and*
> *Flagons of Wine on it.*

The elaborate preparations involve the opening of the Study-curtains: they disclose the 'table prepard' and its 'Flagons of Wine'; four or five foils are brought in by the attendants; Osric, the umpire of the duel, presides over the arrangements. The King and Queen (*and all the state*) enter by one of the Doors, and the Queen sits (the thrones are brought forward and prepared by *officers with Cushions**); last, significantly isolated in the Q2 direction, comes Laertes, already stripped for fencing. During the long entry Horatio helps Hamlet to prepare for the duel.

* See *page 59, above.*

The King in the centre of the Stage brings the two combatants together.

Hamlet's apology to Laertes has caused some heart-burning among his admirers. Doctor Johnson, for instance, is wistful in his unconcealed regret: 'I wish Hamlet had made some other defence; it is unsuitable to the character of a good or a brave man, to shelter himself in falsehood.' Shakespeare's intention, however, can be interpreted thus: Hamlet is more than ever on his guard against his uncle, but he is to be shown as utterly unsuspicious of Laertes as he enters upon the match; to him Laertes is 'a very Noble youth' (V.i.246). Prompted by his mother, and following his own inclination, he seeks the first opportunity to be reconciled to him. He knows and confesses that he has wounded both the young man's **nature** (his natural affection, for Polonius was his father) and his **honour** (especially by the violent intervention at Ophelia's graveside). How is Hamlet to make public excuse for this offence? He certainly did not intend to kill Polonius; the fatal blow was intended for the King, and he was incensed at the time; and when he insulted Laertes in the churchyard, he was distraught by his own 'Tow'ring passion' (V.ii.80). He is still, at this moment, surrounded by his enemies—for the courtiers support the King. And to them he is known to have been mad: **This presence knows . . . how I am punish'd With a sore distraction**; they still do not know, and must not be told, that his madness was pretence. But there is a difference between the antic disposition deliberately assumed for the King and court, and the real instability of temper which has from time to time overwhelmed Hamlet. In conversation with Horatio Hamlet described the loss of his emotional control in a significant phrase: 'to Laertes I forgot my self'. Now he makes again the same precise identification of that distraught humour in which **Hamlet from himself** is **ta'en away**, the mood in which **he's not himself**: only in such a mood could he **wrong Laertes**, and he tells the simple truth when he disclaims any **purpos'd evil**. So we must not think that by his apology he is (in Johnson's phrase) sheltering himself in falsehood.* His **offer'd love** is entirely sincere.

Laertes's response, on the other hand, is anything but ingenuous. He

* See *page 55, above.*

declares himself **satisfied in Nature**—which we know he is not: he is unswervingly bent on avenging his father. And when he goes on to reserve judgement on a point of **Honour,** we cannot be blind to the hypocrisy of one who at this very moment is preparing to commit murder. His hypocrisy is indeed explicit:

> **I do receive your offer'd love like love,**
> **And will not wrong it.**

And when Hamlet generously concedes pre-eminence to Laertes, there is no doubt where, as they get ready for **this Brother's wager,** Shakespeare intends our sympathy to be.

The mechanics of the duel itself are brilliantly contrived, and not for the first time we can wonder at the skill with which in Shakespeare's poetic drama the spoken word of the actors is made to contain the action within itself, so that (almost without stage-directions) we understand the course of events and their dramatic effect upon the characters on the Stage.

The reconciliation apparently made, Osric brings **the Foils**, and while the King engages Hamlet's attention in a discussion of current form, Laertes has an opportunity to reject the foil brought to him and go to the table for another: there he can take the button off and dip the point in his deadly 'Unction'. Hamlet, still suspecting no danger in the friendly match, and eager (in spite of his protestation of inferiority) to show his skill, is content with the first foil he chooses from Osric's armful; presumably, he says, they **have all a length.** Claudius's plan depended, we remember, upon the Prince's 'being remiss, Most generous, and free from all contriving', so that he 'will not peruse the Foils' (IV.vii.134 ff.).

The King prescribes, for the benefit of the assembled company (which includes, of course, the whole playhouse), the expected order of proceedings: the first time Hamlet scores a hit, he will drink his health, and before passing the cup to his nephew drop a pearl (he uses the word **union**, the name given to a pearl of unique quality[31]) into the cup as a gift. When he says **Give me the Cups,** **And let the Kettle to the Trumpets speak . . .,** he is not issuing an order to be carried out there and then, but describing what he intends shall happen, when Hamlet wins a bout. The King's grandiloquent words lead us to anticipate the full resources of the company's sound-effects. The kettle-drum will be echoed by the trumpeter, and he in turn by the **Cannoneer without**: the cannon will speak to **the Heavens** from its lofty position in the Huts, and the sound will re-echo to the **Earth**, the Stage beneath. At **Come, begin**, Claudius sits on his throne beside Gertrude; and, with *Trumpets the while* (the direction is in Q2), Hamlet and Laertes go through the motions of the salute.

[293-297] Osric is one of the **Judges**: Horatio may well be another. They are to **bear a wary eye**. FIRST BOUT: Hamlet claims a hit, Laertes denies it, Hamlet appeals to the judges, and Osric decides in his favour. Laertes is for beginning again, but the King rises to perform the ceremony he has already described. With the cup in one hand and the pearl in the other, he drinks Hamlet's **health**, then drops the pearl (we know, of course, that it is the poison) into the cup, and directs his attendant to give the cup to Hamlet. Immediately, according to the instructions we have heard, the trumpets blow, the drums beat, and the 'Cannoneer without' touches off his powder: the Q2 direction is: *Drum, trumpets and shot. Florish, a peece goes off.* Throughout the prolonged din of the King's 'rouse' (which we heard long ago in the distance from the battlements), Hamlet stands motionless with the poisoned cup in his hand; and our nerves are on edge.

[298-310] SECOND BOUT: Hamlet postpones his drink, handing the cup to an attendant. They engage again; and no doubt Burbage and Sly give an exhibition of skill to satisfy both groundlings and connoisseurs of the art of fence. This time Hamlet's hit is so 'palpable' that Laertes cannot deny it. Hamlet returns to the **Stage-Post** which serves him as combatant's corner, and the Queen rises from her throne and moves to join him there, offering her **Napkin** to wipe the sweat off his face. At her elbow is the cup-bearer, and impulsively she takes the cup from him and drinks good luck to Hamlet. This last exchange between mother and son is both courteous and affectionate. When the King from his throne tries to prevent her from drinking, she insists: **I will my Lord; I pray you pardon me**. There is a hint of hauteur in her rebuff to her lord, a touch of coquettishness, which is ironically

painful in the tragic circumstances of her predicament. The King points the irony explicitly for us: **It is the poison'd Cup, it is too late.** As for Hamlet, he is still not ready to drink; a fencer needs his wits about him; he is all intent upon his match, oblivious of the horror which is developing before his eyes. Laertes, who has retreated to his corner, is close to the King's chair and tries to reassure his confederate that he will hit Hamlet in the next bout; but Claudius has lost confidence, as he sees his plans going all awry. Laertes too, we hear in a whispered *aside*, is shaken with a breath of compunction: **And yet 'tis almost 'gainst my conscience.**

[311-315] THIRD BOUT: Hamlet returns to the fray, exhilarated by his success, in high spirits as we have never seen him in the course of the story, playfully rallying his opponent, his relaxed style of fencing in noticeable contrast with Laertes's anxious tension. Thrust and parry end in deadlock, and Osric pronounces this bout a draw.

[315-324] The dramatic sequel to this third bout is clear from the tone and sense of the next few lines, short as they are. Osric's **Nothing neithe rway** indicates that the bout is over and judged, and we expect an interim, as twice before. Instead, we have Laertes's sudden **Have at you now.** Hamlet has his back turned as he moves to his corner, and Laertes lung esat him; it is plain from what follows that Hamlet is wounded by the unbated point. Astonished at the foul blow, he finds the blood flowing and in fury leaps in to the attack. There is no grace or skill in the ensuing battle, no respect for rule or ceremony: for the Folio stage-direction is explicit: *In scuffling they change Rapiers*: and as the enraged fight continues, the King, with his guilty knowledge, cries: **Part them, they are incens'd.** We know (but Hamlet does not) that Laertes is fighting for his life: there is poison on the point of the rapier he has lost to Hamlet. The double climax comes suddenly. As Osric sees the Queen fall, Horatio calls out: **They bleed on both sides**; the poisoned blade has penetrated Laertes's guard.

Laertes, supported by Osric, confesses himself to be killed, **justly**, with his own treachery, and we barely have time to wonder how far Osric has been an accomplice, when Hamlet becomes aware of his mother's collapse. Claudius, in a desperate and vain attempt to conceal the crime of the poisoned cup, tries to pretend that she is faint at the sight of blood. But she points to the cup, now standing on the table: **Oh my dear Hamlet** (she looks in the end, not to her husband, but to her son), **the drink, the drink, I am poison'd.**

[325-334] Still unaware of his own plight, Hamlet clamours to have the door locked (we hear the heavy bolts being shot beyond the Study), and turns to seek out the treachery. But **it is here Hamlet . . . No Medicine in the world can do thee good . . .** In measured terms, with relentless clarity, Laertes reveals the whole grim truth:

> **The Treacherous Instrument is in thy hand,**
> **Unbated and envenom'd . . .**
> **. . . Thy Mother's poison'd . . .**

(and the dying man, since he **can no more**, points out the arch-criminal)

> **. . . the King, the King's to blame.**

[335-341] So now the interim is short indeed—not half an hour to live. But the instrument is in Hamlet's hand, there's poison too on the point ('And is't not to be damn'd To let this Canker of our nature come Infurther evil?')—**Then venom to thy work.** The courtiers, bewildered and panic-stricken, still cling to their loyalty: to strike the King is **Treason.** * But Hamlet will not be stopped now, he shoulders aside the half-hearted defenders, forces the wounded King against the table and thrusts the poisoned cup between his lips. Prosser's argument that 'Hamlet is guilty of manslaughter, not premeditated murder' is convincing in the study, but not on the stage; in the continuous action of the play, the death of Claudius is the achievement of the vow made by Hamlet to his father's Ghost. Raking the climax of achieved vengeance with his mordant wit, he demands **Is thy Union here?** The union, the pearl, was the poison in the cup. The union too of his Uncle with his mother is here, in death. **Follow my Mother.**

[341-363] The death of Laertes would pass almost unnoticed, a parenthesis between the deaths of the two mighty opposites. But Shakespeare does not let us forget that here is the extinction of the

* See *pages* 89–90, *above.*

house of Polonius; and yet he gives to Laertes a generosity at his death the greater in contrast to the baseness of his stratagem: calling his adversary **Noble** (an epithet echoed later by Horatio), he offers an exchange of **forgiveness**:

> **Mine and my Father's death come not upon thee,**
> **Nor thine on me.**

The young man's dying acknowledgement of Hamlet's nobility is a cardinal point in Shakespeare's plan, and he does not mean us to overlook this moment of truth.

Hamlet's dying speeches have, like most of Shakespeare's mature writing, a sustained musical structure, carefully calculated in variety of tempo, volume and colour. No doubt the poet hoped that Burbage would resist the temptation to stretch, as great tragedians will, such cadences to unmetrical length. Here (as we have noted before) there is a running refrain to knit the passage together: **I am dead, Horatio . . . Horatio, I am dead . . . O God, Horatio** (where the rhythm becomes more urgent) **. . . O I die, Horatio.** The address to the hostile court, who now **look pale, and tremble at this chance**, is a public utterance (made perhaps from a position on or near the King's throne). The conditions of the daylit theatre give special point to the metaphor in which Hamlet addresses the court **that are but Mutes or audience to this act**. Audience and actors are in the same neutral light: the metaphor becomes reality, and Hamlet's public words are directed to the whole playhouse. The court are only 'audience to this act'; and conversely, we in the audience are silent partakers of the scene on the Stage. But the effort taxes too much the strength of the dying man: **oh I could tell you** is urgent, and we begin to realise that to the world Hamlet seems still a madman and a murderer. But **this fell Sergeant death Is strict in his Arrest**, and so Horatio, the faithful friend, must set the record right.

And then with a stroke of the unpredictable, Shakespeare shatters the stillness of the scene in a moment of violence. Horatio, of all people, whose blood and judgement are so well commingled, the man that is not passion's slave, forgets his nature, his duty, his philosophy, and tries to kill himself. There is a struggle, which further taxes Hamlet's ebbing strength; but his urgent need overcomes his friend's faltering purpose, and the poisoned cup (with **yet some Liquor left**) falls to the floor. Remembering the recurrent expressions of Hamlet's world-weariness, we can measure the depth of feeling in his plea:

Absent thee from felicity awhile.

[363-374]   Once more we are taken unawares by the unexpected. A marching drum is heard in the distance: the Folio's stage-direction is: *March afarre off, and shout within.* The firing of guns is interpreted for us as a **warlike volley.** Once again the unexpected proves to be the inevitable, the one circumstance that can justly complete the grand architecture of this huge play. **Young Fortinbras** has come back from Poland in triumph, and the guns greet **th'Ambassadors of England** whom he has encountered by the way. There is no time to hear **the News from England**—what does it matter?—but Hamlet's last thought is for the succession to the throne of Denmark: Fortinbras is the man. **The rest is silence.** Before the newcomers intrude, Horatio's brief farewell gives a moment of poignant intimacy, unmistakably echoing the Liturgy for the Dead: *in paradisum deducant te angeli.*[32]

[375-417]   The heavy bolts beyond the Study are heard again, as the door from the outside world is opened. The *coda* is public, and the main theme of it Hamlet's reputation. We note in passing the expected fate of Rosencrantz and Guildenstern. But the focus of interest is divided between the warrior Prince Fortinbras, who assumes command, and the mourning scholar Horatio who, with a new assurance bred of the solemn urgency of Hamlet's last commission, claims the right to make his friend's funeral oration; the preliminary account of what he intends to say serves as a summary of the play's action: he will speak

> **Of carnal, bloody, and unnatural acts,**
> **Of accidental judgements, casual slaughters,**
> **Of deaths put on by cunning and forc'd cause,**
> **And in this upshot purposes mistook**
> **Fall'n on the Inventors' heads.**

His acknowledgement of Fortinbras's claim has the authority of Hamlet's 'dying voice'. Fortinbras's epilogue assures us, if we need assurance, that Hamlet **was likely, had he been put on, To have prov'd most royally.** He is to be borne **like a Soldier to the Stage** —a military funeral—and Fortinbras's **four Captains** carry his body into the Study, as the curtains close on **this quarry** of **so many Princes.**

It may be that, while the audience is still applauding the end of the play, the curtains of the Chamber part once again, to show us the Prince's body **high on a stage . . . placed to the view.** Certainly, as the stage-direction of the Folio makes plain, Fortinbras's order, **Go, bid the Soldiers shoot,** is immediately obeyed: the last sound we hear in the play comes from the Huts above the Heavens: *after the which, a Peale of Ordenance are shot off.*

NOTES

Page 27

1 The practice is noted by Percy Simpson, *Shakespeare's England*, vol. II, 280. Among other examples he quotes the opening line of I HENRY VI: 'Hung be the heavens with black'. The metaphor, drawn like so many of Shakespeare's from the playhouse itself, is chosen to symbolise the tragedy of Henry the Fifth's premature death.

Page 29

2 Eleanor Prosser, *Hamlet and Revenge*, 98 f., suggests that 'the spirit is offended only when Horatio charges it "by heaven" to speak'. This interpretation is a cardinal element in her argument that Shakespeare's audiences would have regarded the Ghost as demonic; the course of private revenge which the Ghost enjoins upon Hamlet, she argues, is to be considered as damnable rather than as a sacred duty; only in the closing scenes of the play does Hamlet escape the danger to his soul: 'he has fought his way out of Hell'. It is not possible here to do justice to Miss Prosser's argument; for the argument itself and the many insights that arise out of it, the reader can do no better than to turn to her book.

But it is appropriate for our purpose to consider the presentation of the Ghost in performance on the stage. The dilemma suffered by Hamlet during the first part of the play is clear: is the Ghost a devil or truly the spirit of the old King? Hamlet himself is made to express this dilemma. He speaks of the first possibility, that the Ghost is malignant, to Horatio and the soldiers ('if it assume my noble Father's person . . .', I.ii.243). Almost immediately afterwards, in the security of soliloquy, he gives words to the second possibility, that the Ghost is truly what it seems ('My Father's Spirit in Arms?', I.ii.254). But it is not only to Hamlet, blinded by passion, that this second possibility appears a real one. Horatio, right up to the moment of 'Heavens secure him' (I.v.113), fears chiefly the Ghost's malignancy; but after that scene Shakespeare wishes it to

143

appear that Horatio too, now in Hamlet's confidence, believes the proving of Claudius's guilt to be a proper test of the Ghost's intentions. It would have been easy enough, before or after the Mouse-trap play, for Shakespeare to make Horatio warn Hamlet, as Banquo warns Macbeth, that 'oftentimes, to win us to our harm, The Instruments of Darkness tell us Truths': he does not do so. By whatever standards a reader, at leisure and in perspective, may judge the morality of private revenge, it must appear to the audience in the playhouse that Hamlet has reason to feel his revenge as an inescapable duty; it must appear too that Horatio has no reason to disagree. While the play is in progress, the hellish provenance of the Ghost is not as indisputable as Prosser suggests.

She is right, certainly, to stress the disquiet and terror of the opening scenes, the sense of potential evil: 'the Spirit that I have seen May be the Devil'. The Ghost is certainly no intoning saint, and any attempt to curtail or under-stress his imagery of the terrors of Hell would reduce the essential complexity of the dilemma. But Shakespeare has left hints enough that this is not the only emphasis he requires. The Ghost is 'fair' as well as 'warlike', 'stately', 'solemn', 'majestical'; it frowns 'more in sorrow than in anger'; it has a 'courteous action'. Again and again its total resemblance to Hamlet's father is stressed, and the old King is spoken of always in terms of nobility: the palpable contra-diction of a diabolical demeanour would be absurd. It may be that Prosser is right in saying that the Ghost is offended because Horatio calls upon Heaven to help him, but we must remember that the name and the powers of Heaven are on at least two other occasions invoked in the presence of the Ghost without its seeming offended (I.iv.39; I.v.24; III.iv.103 f.). Above all, when the Ghost finally speaks, the impact of its words on Hamlet (and on us) is less of terror than of pathos: the powerful sensuality Prosser observes in the language of the Ghost suggests not the presence of evil but intense (and human) suffering.

While it is possible that, in detachment, audiences may regard the Ghost as demonic and Hamlet's course of action as damnable, any attempt to force them to do so by simplifying the presentation of the Ghost is surely mistaken. Even in the first scene Horatio's conjurations (I.i.128 ff.) imply a greater un-certainty about the Ghost's nature and purpose than Prosser admits. And as to the question of Hamlet's dedication to private revenge, and his identification of patient suffering with cowardice, we should remember that Hamlet is not Macbeth; his course of action is not presented to us as explicitly evil. Though Shakespeare undoubtedly raises moral questions, he asks from us not judgement but human understanding.

Page 40

3 Such descriptions are those of Benvolio (ROMEO AND JULIET, III.i.157 ff.), Puck (A MIDSUMMER NIGHT'S DREAM, III.ii.6 ff.), and Iachimo (CYMBELINE, II.iv.66 ff.). Iachimo's description of Imogen to Posthumus, though deliberately false in its central circumstance, reinforces with much addition of vivid detail the picture he has already sketched for us in soliloquy as he emerges from the trunk in her bed-chamber (II.ii.11 ff.).

Page 49

4 Charlton Hinman, in his Introduction to the Norton Facsimile, xvii, explains why the Folio's printing of **& prey on Garbage** (included in a single line of type with the preceding line) is not to be considered as evidence against Shakespeare's deliberate intention to produce a short line. There is perhaps another climactic short line in the passage: **To those of mine**. Although both Q2 and the Folio combine the words with the succeeding line (**But Virtue, as it never will be moved**), the rhythm suggests strongly that they should be isolated.

Page 51

5 But for another view see Martin Holmes, *The Guns of Elsinore*, 79.

Page 53

6 Dover Wilson (*What Happens in HAMLET*, 79) suggests that Hamlet deliberately invokes Saint Patrick, the keeper of Purgatory, by way of warning Horatio that 'it is an honest ghost'; from this he deduces that Marcellus is not to hear the revelation. The reader is referred to his analysis of the scene, which, though it may seem too rational an interpretation of Hamlet's 'whirling words', is perfectly feasible on the stage.

Page 55

7 Prosser, 149, writes: 'If I were directing the play, I would have Hamlet take his cue from Horatio's reaction to his hysterical levity. . . . Hamlet realizes that the course he has chosen—acting alone and under intense emotional stress—is dangerous. Knowing himself, he realizes that he may act oddly and picks up the suggestion implicit in Horatio's puzzled response to his erratic behaviour.' Prosser goes on to point out that in Shakespeare's day, 'antic' did not mean 'mad', but 'grotesque' or 'ludicrous'; it was a commonly used epithet for Death.

Page 61

8 M. C. Bradbrook, *The Growth and Structure of Elizabethan Comedy*, 45, has the interesting comment: 'His letter to Ophelia, opening in a decorous manner "To the celestial and my soul's idol, the most beautified Ophelia", becomes suddenly tender, familiar, ironical—in the personal accent of wit and pain.'

Page 62

9 *What Happens in HAMLET*, 106 ff.

Page 64

10 It is possible that we are intended to feel (as Dover Wilson suggests, *What Happens in HAMLET*, 114 ff.) that Claudius suspects Hamlet of designs upon the throne, and that it is convenient for Hamlet's purpose to foster this belief. The most specific indication of this purpose appears in III.ii.361: 'Sir I lack Advancement'. In II.ii we have only hints—the emphasis upon the word 'ambition' and Hamlet's apologies, 'I am most dreadfully attended' and 'Beggar that I am'—and it is interesting that the lines which contain these hints are omitted in Q2. Whether or not the theme of thwarted ambition is as clearly discernible as Dover Wilson suggests, the hints here certainly contribute to the sense of a battle of wits between Hamlet and the spies.

Page 65

11 Prosser, 150.

Page 67

12 Martin Holmes, 93 f., makes the suggestion that 'Hamlet's commentary on the unnamed play is quite an acceptable assessment of TROILUS AND CRESSIDA'. The chronological evidence is confused: it is at least possible that, while he was writing HAMLET, Shakespeare had already in mind the material for the other play. Cf. the curious reference to Mark Antony in MACBETH, III.i.55 ff.

Page 72

13 In his play, *Rosencrantz and Guildenstern are Dead*, Tom Stoppard develops the theme of Hamlet's ruthless manipulation of the unfortunate spies. They carefully practise for their first interview with him by way of an elaborate game of question and answer, designed to trap him into some confession. In the event the tables are turned, and they admit to themselves what they cannot admit to the King: 'Twenty-seven questions he got out in ten minutes, and answered three. . . . Six rhetorical and two repetition, leaving nineteen of

which we answered fifteen. And what did we get in return? He's depressed!
... Denmark's a prison and he'd rather live in a nutshell; some shadow-play
about the nature of ambition. . . .'

Page 73

14 This suggested treatment of *lines* 56–60 is of course mere conjecture, and
may seem to the traditionalists a reckless one. Professor James Sandoe draws
our attention to the fact that Hardin Craig thirty or so years ago observed that
'To be or not to be . . .' was closely paraphrased from a contemporary consideration of suicide. *Hamlet's Book*, by Hardin Craig, can be found in the Huntington
Library Bulletin, no. 6 (November, 1934), 17–37. Cardan's *De Consolatione*
is the work in question. See also K. Muir, *Shakespeare's Sources*, vol. I, 121 f.
Sandoe adds that William Thornton was probably the first actor to pick up
the hint, while touring with a repertory company in California in 1930–5,
and manage this scene as reading from, and speculation upon, a book-in-hand.
Consideration of the question of Hamlet's book still continues: see an article
by W. G. Bebbington in *T.L.S.* for 20 March 1969, and subsequent correspondence. The position of the phrase 'in the mind', looking forward to 'to
suffer' rather than backward to ' 'tis Nobler', suggests a Latin order of words.
The phrase 'Sea of troubles', which has disturbed those commentators who
take exception to the use of mixed metaphor, is a commonplace of Greek
tragedy. To begin from Hamlet's book does not alter the tenour of the rest
of the soliloquy, and in practice it establishes the mood of gentle reflection
which is such an effective contrast to the passionate violence of Hamlet's last
utterance, and which prepares us for the quiet opening moment of his scene
with Ophelia.

Page 75

15 Prosser (163 f.), in her interesting analysis of 'To be or not to be', observes
this correspondence between 'the two great soliloquies of moral choice', but
she later argues (205 ff.) that the second of them was not intended by Shakespeare to be part of his final version of the play.

16 Coghill, *Shakespeare's Professional Skills*, 158.

Page 76

17 Coghill, 16 ff.

Page 79

18 Discussing the growth of fastidiousness in Shakespeare's own writing, D. P. Young in *Something of Great Constancy*, 34–42, gives many examples of the kind of conventions which Shakespeare was attacking, even when he wrote A MIDSUMMER NIGHT'S DREAM. He points out that 'Shakespeare's rival theater was still presenting plays in the Senecan style if not in Cambises' vein. It was still possible in 1614, if we are to believe the prologue to *Bartholomew Fair*, to find those "who swear *Ieronimo* and *Andronicus* are the best plays yet".'

Page 82

19 That all the persons on the stage watch the Dumb Show is the opinion of Granville-Barker, and the reader is referred to his exposition of the scene in his *Preface*, 98 ff., and especially to his footnote (105 f.) in which he argues against the view of Dover Wilson, who thinks that the King does not see the Dumb Show.

Page 84

20 Martin Holmes, 122 f., argues that the part of Lucianus was not performed by the First Player as it has so often been upon the stage; Hamlet would not abuse his 'old friend' in public; nor would the First Player, with a performance which is 'overdone or come tardy off', deserve such abuse.

Page 90

21 The most celebrated discussion of tyrannicide had appeared in the pamphlet *Vindiciae contra Tyrannos*, perhaps by Duplessis-Mornay. It is described by Lord Acton as 'the beginning of the literature of revolution'.

Page 92

22 There are parallels to this dialectical treatment of the struggle for repentance in certain passages of Marlowe's *Doctor Faustus*, a play which explores the use of dialectic on the stage in several different forms: most akin to Claudius's soliloquy are the speeches beginning 'Now, Faustus, must thou needs be damned . . .' and 'My heart's so hardened I cannot repent'.

Page 97

23 There is not space in this volume to deal as extensively as they deserve with Shakespeare's image-patterns. The studies of imagery by Caroline Spurgeon, Wolfgang Clemen and others have greatly added to our insight into Shakespeare's craft as a poet and into the workings of his imagination;

they have also contributed (and this is closer to the purpose of the present study) to an understanding of the methods by which the poetic drama achieves its ends. Both particular visual and psychological effects, and the total impact of the play, the creation of its 'world', depend partly on the pervasive imagery examined by Spurgeon. The reader is especially referred to Clemen's *The Development of Shakespeare's Imagery*, which gives a full discussion of Shakespeare's use of imagery as a *dramatic* weapon.

Page 102

24 It is interesting that the reporter, whose eccentric memory seems to underly the text of the First Quarto, remembered especially a volleying of 'son' and 'father' between Claudius and Hamlet. The sequence is as follows: 'Now sonne Hamlet, where is this dead body? . . . Father, your fatte King, and your leane Beggar . . . Nothing father, but to tell you, how a King May go a progresse . . . But sonne *Hamlet*, where is this body? . . . Father, you had best looke in the other partes below For him . . . Well sonne *Hamlet*, we in care of you . . . farewel mother.—Your loving father, *Hamlet*.—My mother I say: you married my mother, My mother is your wife, man and wife is one flesh, And so (my mother) farewel: for England hoe.' For all the confusion of the scene, it looks as if the reporter had felt the reminiscence in this dialogue of Claudius's flattering solicitude of I.ii and Hamlet's resentment: 'I am too much in the sonne'.

Page 106

25 Prosser, 205 ff., has a radically different interpretation, and argues that the soliloquy was not intended by Shakespeare as part of his final version of the play.

Page 108

26 E. W. Naylor in *Shakespeare and Music* (and more fully in *Shakespeare Music*) provides contemporary tunes for Ophelia's songs, most of them based upon the old air *Walsingham*. Richmond Noble (*Shakespeare's Use of Song*, 119) has some interesting comments on the content and dramatic relevance of these songs.

Page 126

27 'It was customary for the mourners to carry small branches of bay, rosemary, or other evergreens as emblems of the soul's immortality, which they threw into the grave' (*Shakespeare's England*, II.149).

Page 127

28 For an interesting discussion of the possibility of 'simultaneous speech' in this scene, see R. Flatter, *Shakespeare's Producing Hand*, 61 ff.

Page 131

29 The hint is so interpreted by Dover Wilson: see his note *ad loc.*

Page 133

30 The reader is referred to Dover Wilson's explanation of the terms of the wager, in his note on V.ii.166–8. We have accepted Dover Wilson's view, but an interesting alternative can be found in *The Odds on Hamlet* by Evert Sprinchorn (*The American Statistician*, December 1970). He suggests that the duel is to consist of a maximum of 12 bouts, and that Laertes can win only by scoring 3 hits in succession. 'Hamlet, on the other hand, need only keep Laertes from scoring three in a row. Or, of course, he can score three in a row himself. Once these conditions have been established, some of the dialogue and much of the action in the last part of the play can be seen in a new light.' It is interesting that, as the duel falls out, Hamlet scores the first two hits; Laertes's agitation and Claudius's determination that Hamlet should drink of the poisoned cup are both especially plausible if we believe that another point in Hamlet's favour would conclude the match, and that Laertes would not have a chance to inflict his poisoned blow.

Page 136

31 Instead of the Folio's 'union', Q2 prints 'Onixe', although it has 'pearle' at *line* 275: it looks as if the word-play at *line* 340 escaped the printer's understanding, and (surprisingly) Pope too accepts 'Onixe'.

Page 141

32 See Christopher Devlin, *Hamlet's Divinity*, 42.